JOY with HONEY

JOY with HONEY

By Doris Mech

Illustrations: Cover, title pages & bees by Vicki Dorsey
All others by Dick Markle

Women's Aglow Fellowship, P.O. Box I, Lynnwood, WA 98036 USA

The biblical references in this book are taken from the King James
Version of the Bible, unless otherwise noted: TLB, The Living Bible;
TAB, The Amplified Bible.

Table of Contents

Breakfast 18

Beverages 26

Breads 34

Salads & Dressings 54

Meats & Vegetables 66

Cakes 80

Pies 90

Cookies 100

Desserts 108

Canning with Honey 120

Index 132

Acknowledgements

Dedicated to my husband Don and my daughter Deena. I am most thankful for their patience as I tested each recipe on them. Without their encouragement this book would have been impossible.

Forward

For centuries honey has been an important food. The Bible mentions honey frequently. In fact, Caanan was described as a land flowing with milk and honey. Honey was valued both as a food and as a commodity of trade.

An excellent source of energy, honey is a natural when it comes to good home cooking. You'll find that baked goods will stay moister when you use honey as a sweetener. Honey is hygroscopic in nature, meaning that it draws moisture from the air. Your bread, cake, or cookies will not dry out as fast as those made without honey. However, as tasty as they are, your baked goods made with honey may not be around long enough to make the hygroscopic test!

Honey also affects the texture of baked goods. Cakes and quick breads will be noticeably heavier and moister. Any food made with honey will continue to improve in flavor after baking and will be even better the second day; for this reason honey-baked goods make excellent gifts and are especially suitable for mailing long distances.

The flavor of honey is different than that of sugar. Baked goods made with honey may not taste as sweet as those made with sugar. Your family may need a period of adjustment to get used to the subtler sweetness of honey products.

In order to produce one pound of honey, an individual bee would have to fly a distance equal to one and one-third trips around the world. It's a fact that honey bees are used to pollinate crops worth over a billion dollars per year in the United States. Over ninety crops are dependent upon the honey bee for pollination. So, you see, the little busy honey bee not only produces delicious honey for us to use, but also is invaluable to the agricultural economy around the world.

Doris Mech

Flavors of Honey

There are several hundred varieties of honey produced in different parts of the world. The United States alone produces over 200 kinds. The commonest honey on sale in the USA is clover honey. It accounts for about 70% of all honey sales.

Many travelers enjoy purchasing honey unique to a given geographic area: orange blossom honey from California, buckwheat honey from New York state, tupelo honey from Florida, or fireweed honey from Washington state. To the seasoned traveler, taking a small jar of honey home is like taking home a little part of the land itself.

There are strong flavored honeys and delicately flavored honeys, distinctively floral honeys, and even fruity flavored honeys. The delightful difference is due not only to taste, but also in a large extent to odor. One of the most heavenly scents on earth is experienced when one walks into a "honey house" when the beekeeper is extracting fresh honey from the comb.

"But don't you have any 'bee' honey?" This question was recently asked at our honey stand in Seattle's famous Pike Place Market. "Yes," we had to chuckle, "it's all honey made by the bees." The name given to each honey is related to the predominate blossoms the honey bees have been working. A given type may vary slightly from year to year, depending on weather conditions, but the honey connoisseur can distinguish the difference.

In the greater Puget Sound area of Washington state, we produce some of the most delicious honeys to be found anywhere. They include: **maple honey** (robust and woodsy, distinct in flavor), **blackberry honey** (pleasantly mild honey with a fruity overtone), **snowberry honey** (delightfully mild, with a slight tang!), **fireweed honey** (delicately light), **cascade wildflower** (dark, and pleasingly strong), and **star thistle** (very light and delicate, with only a slight aftertaste). Personal favorites are a matter of taste.

More about Honey

How can I buy honey?

1, 2, 3, 5, or 12-lb. jars. A 12-oz. jar equals one standard 8-oz. measuring cup, a 3-lb. can equals 4 cups, and a 5-lb. can equals 6 2/3 cups.

Crystallized forms of honey, often called **creamed honey, spun honey,** or **honey butter** are readily available. They are the right consistency for spreading on toast.

Other types of honey which are more difficult to find are: **comb honey,** packed in square boxes; **chunk honey** packed in jars with liquid honey surrounding the comb; **cut comb honey** cut in small chunks and wrapped in individual cellophane-covered cartons; **cappings and honey,** another rare treat, consisting of a delicious combination of beeswax (cut off the top of the honey comb) and raw honey. It can be chewed like candy or used as a spread.

How should I store honey?

Honey keeps best when stored in a tightly covered container in your cupboard. If you buy honey in large quantities, you many want to store it in several small containers. Do not refrigerate honey since this accelerates the granulation. Freezing will not injure honey, however. Honey should never be over-heated because this will change its flavor and also destroy beneficial enzymes and other nutrients.

What if my honey crystalizes?

The honey used for the recipes in this book is in the natural liquid form, sometimes also called extracted honey. If your jar of honey starts to granulate, it is not spoiled in any way. This just means that the enzymes have begun a crystalization process. To liquify the honey again, simply place the closed jar in warm (not hot) water until all of the crystals melt. Another way is to put the jar of granulated honey in a warm oven (about 100 degrees) until it is liquified.

How do I measure honey?

Whenever you use honey in cooking, measure it in a cup moistened with oil or melted butter. This allows the honey to slide right out without any sticky scraping. Better yet, if the recipe calls for oil, measure the oil first in the same cup as the honey.

Will my baked goods have the same volume with honey?

In baking cakes and cookies, volume will be increased if the honey is added to the batter in a continuous fine stream. Continue beating while you add the honey.

How do I convert recipes to use honey?

The question often arises as to how to convert recipes from sugar to honey. There is no simple hard and fast rule, but I will give a few tips to you adventurous cooks.

In quick breads, cakes or cookies the general rule is to substitute two-thirds cup honey for each cup sugar. Also, reduce the amount of liquid by one-quarter cup for each cup of honey used. You will also need to add a little more leavening agent — usually one-half teaspoon baking soda for each cup of honey used. This helps neutralize honey's natural acidity. In addition, remember to lower the baking temperature 25 degrees because goods baked with honey tend to brown faster.

When only small amounts of sweetener are used such as in yeast breads or salad dressing, you do not need to adjust the recipe.

In some recipes you can use less honey. In most fruit pies, for example, use one-fourth cup less honey than sugar, but increase the thickening agent by one-half (flour, cornstarch, eggs, tapioca, gelatin). Honey does have more of a sweetening power. In addition, it brings out the natural flavors of fruit.

Know Your Ingredients

If you're new to the realm of natural foods there will be some ingredients in **JOY WITH HONEY** that you'll want to get acquainted with. For your information, we have included a little helpful information on these natural foods that are not readily available in the supermarket.

AGAR - AGAR

Agar-agar, a jelling agent that comes from seaweed, is rich in minerals from the ocean. It is also good for low-protein diets. Agar-agar comes in different forms: flaked, granulated, powder or cake form. We have used the **flaked** agar-agar in Apple Jelly.

BEE POLLEN

Bee pollen is a wondrously rich and nutritious food which is produced by the flowers and gathered by the bees. Beekeepers collect it by making the worker bees crawl across a screen as they enter their hive. It is then dehydrated and sorted by hand. It comes in its original pellet form — from the bee's knees. It is also available in powdered or pill form or in a mixture with honey. We have used the natural **pellet form** of bee pollen in the following recipes: HONEY BEE PEANUT BUTTER SANDWICH, ENERGY BARS, BANANA MANNA, and MANNA BARS.

BRAN (UNPROCESSED MILLER'S BRAN)

Please do not confuse this with Bran Flakes Cereal from the supermarket. The results can be disastrous! Unprocessed Miller's Bran has no sugar, salt or any additives at all. It's just plain bran from the outer bran layers of the wheat berry. Bran provides us with vitally needed roughage and fiber in our diets. You can add one or two tablespoons of bran to meat loaf, granola, casseroles, or any baked goods. Or, for more bran, try our BRAN MUFFINS.

CAROB

Carob is a powder which resembles chocolate in taste. It comes from the long brown pods of the carob tree, which is a member of the locust family. The pods are known to some as "St. John's Bread" because they were said to have sustained John the Baptist in the Wilderness. The best edible varieties grow in the countries near the Mediterranean Sea. The nicest thing about carob, besides its delicate flavor, is the fact that it's lower in fat and free from stimulants. (Chocolate contains theobromine, a stimulant similar to caffeine.) Carob is rich in minerals. It also is high in Vitamin A and Niacin, with traces of Vitamin B1 and B2. We use both carob powder and carob chips. Look for recipes in the cake, beverage, dessert and cookie sections.

Hint: 3 T. carob & 2 T. water = 1 square of chocolate

CHAMOMILE

Chamomile or camomile is an old-fashioned herb tea. It is made from the blossoms of Anthemis nobilis, sometimes called Ground Apple or Whig Plant. Do you remember the story of Peter Rabbit? After having a very upsetting day, he was sent to bed with a cup of chamomile tea. If you have a little garden spot you can grow your own tea! It's an excellent table tea as well as being beneficial to the body. Try our recipe for DEEP SLEEP TEA with chamomile.

COCONUT (UNSWEETENED)

This is just plain finely grated coconut, which has been dried. It's plenty sweet naturally. Why not enjoy it in its own state? It's delicious sprinkled on top of fruit salad. We use it extensively in baking cookies, desserts, and in Coconut Frosting, Coconut Pie Shell and Marilyn's Homemade Granola.

TAPIOCA FLOUR

Tapioca flour, sometimes referred to as "tapioca starch," is derived from the large fleshy root of the cassava plant, a shrub cultivated in tropical America and in the West Indies. Natives form the nutritious starch into cakes called cassava-bread. Our familiar Minute Tapioca and Pearl Tapioca come from the same plant. Tapioca flour or tapioca starch can be purchased in Oriental food stores. It is an excellent thickening agent which we have used in HONEY BEE SUNSHINE PRESERVES.

NON-INSTANT POWDERED MILK

The notable difference between instant powdered milk and non-instant is texture. Non-instant powdered milk is as fine as face powder. It is beautifully white and has a mild, delicate taste and odor. It is very adaptable to cooking, for it mixes readily with other dry ingredients and will not become lumpy when you stir it in. It makes a nice coating for "sweets" in lieu of rolling in powdered sugar. (See the NO-BAKE APPLE COOKIES.) Be sure to store your non-instant powdered milk in an air-tight container, as it can pick up a lot of moisture from the air and become solidified.

WHEAT GERM

A kernel of wheat can be divided approximately into three main parts as follows: 84 percent endosperm, 14 percent bran layers, and 2 percent wheat germ. The tiny wheat germ is the embryo or live part of the kernel which is capable of sprouting and growing a new plant. The highest concentration of B vitamins are found in the wheat germ. In the process of milling white flour, the bran layers and the wheat germ are discarded, leaving the endosperm — the starchy center of the wheat. But, in discarding the bran and the germ we lose 95% of the thiamine (vitamin B1), 65 % of the riboflavin (vitamin B2), 85% of the niacin, 90% of the pyridoxin (vitamin B6), 70% of the iron and nearly all of the oil soluble nutrients, notably vitamin E. When flour is milled without the separation made, the result is called "whole wheat," "entire wheat," or "graham." If you are not consuming a lot of whole wheat in your diet, wheat germ is a sensible supple-ment. But please remember, it is perishable, so keep it refrigerated. Toasted wheat germ is less perishable than fresh, but not quite as nutritious. You can add a couple tablespoons of wheat germ to any bread recipe. We have used ¾ cup of it in the GRANOLA DE LUXE.

SOURDOUGH

"LORD, thou hast been our dwelling place in all generations. Before the mountains were brought forth, or ever thou hadst formed the earth and the world, even from everlasting to everlasting, thou art God" (Ps. 90:1, 2).

The old timers in the Alaskan wilderness carried a little crock of yeasty sourdough starter with them. From this starter, they would mix up their traditionally tangy pancakes or bread. The sourdough starter was kept "alive" year after year. Each time a little was used from the crock, a little more flour and water would be added, and the starter would continue to "work." Some of you may be fortunate to have a sourdough starter that originated with the old timers in Alaska. In their tradition of hospitality, the sourdough

was often divided and the precious starter shared with a friend. Because of its history and tradition, sourdough cookery has a certain nostalgia, a certain hearty homemade quality. You will enjoy all of the sourdough recipes included in **JOY WITH HONEY: SOURDOUGH PANCAKES, GRANDMA'S LITTLE HONEY BUNS, and SOURDOUGH CAROB CAKE.**

The best way to start your own sourdough pot is to find someone who will share her "starter" with you. But if there doesn't happen to be a sourdough baker among your friends, you can start one in your own kitchen. Mix together in a crock or cookie jar:

2 cups flour

½ tsp. dry yeast dissolved in

1½ cups lukewarm water

1½ tsp. salt

3 Tbsp. sugar

Keep the crock covered and allow it to sit for two or three days in a fairly warm place. Stir once or twice daily. Now you have your starter. It should be kept in the refrigerator and taken out the night before you want to use from it. Since you never want to use up all the starter, you must always add flour and water to it the night before you use it. Add about twice as much flour as water. You can use either white or wholewheat flour, but wholewheat is especially good with pancakes. Don't fill the crock too full when mixing the flour and water the night before, or the next morning you'll find it has worked its way right out of the crock and all over your cabinet! You should use your starter at least once every two weeks.

OVEN TEMPERATURE

	Celsius (C)	Fahrenheit (F)
very slow	120°-135°	250°-275°
slow	150°-165°	300°-325°
moderate	175°-190°	350°-375°
hot	205°-220°	400°-425°
very hot	230°-245°	450°-475°

TEMPERATURE

Celsius (C)	Fahrenheit (F)
0°	32°
100°	212°
37°	98.6°

METRIC SYMBOLS

COMMON UNIT	MEASUREMENT
meter (m)	length and distance
gram (g)	weight
liter (L)	volume
Celsius (C)	temperature

Prefixes are placed at the beginning of the unit to tell the size of the common unit.

PREFIX	MEANING
kilo (k)	1,000 x common unit
centi (c)	.01 or 1/100 x common unit
milli (m)	.001 or 1/1000 x common unit

When common units and prefixes are combined, measurements larger or smaller than a unit may be shown.

PREFIX	UNIT	MEASUREMENT
kilo	gram	kilogram 1,000 x gram
centi	meter	centimeter 1/100 x meter
mili	liter	mililiter 1/1000 x liter

The symbols will be used rather than spelling out the whole word. Thus 3 milliliters becomes 3 ml. and 2 kilograms becomes 2 kg.

METRIC CONVERSION

	when you know	you can find	if you multiply by
weight is	ounces	grams	28
measured in grams (G)	pounds	kilograms	0.45
1 gram 1/28 ounce	grams	ounces	0.035
1/1000 kilogram	kilograms	pounds	2.2
liquid volume is measured in liters (L)	ounces	milliliters	30
1 liter 1.06 quarts	pints	liters	0.47
	quarts	liters	0.95
	gallons	liters	3.8
	milliliters	ounces	0.034
	liters	pints	2.1
	liters	quarts	1.06
	liters	gallons	0.26

Breakfast

GRANOLA DELUXE

"Great is His faithfulness; His lovingkindness begins afresh each day" (Lam. 3:23 TLB).

Oven: 250°   Yield: about 12 servings

2½ cups oatmeal (dry)
½ cup 40% bran flakes cereal
¾ cup sesame seeds
¾ cup wheat germ
½ cup soy flour
½ cup non-instant dry milk
½ cup raw cashew nuts, broken pieces
½ cup raw sunflower seeds
½ cup vegetable oil
½ cup honey
½ cup dates, finely chopped
½ cup raisins

In a large mixing bowl combine the oatmeal with the bran flakes, sesame seeds, wheat germ, soy flour, dry milk, nuts and sunflower seeds. In a small mixing bowl measure out the oil and honey, then beat together until smooth. Pour the honey-oil mixture over the dry ingredients. Stir with a large wooden spoon until fairly well mixed. Then remove your rings and finish mixing very thoroughly with your hands. Pour out into a 9"x13" baking pan and bake for 50 to 55 minutes or until light golden brown in color, stirring every 15 minutes. Immediately fold in the dried fruit while the mixture is still warm. Cool completely; then store in glass jars with tight lids to preserve its crunchy freshness.

Variations: There are endless opportunities for you to be creative with this recipe. Use peanuts, almonds, or walnuts in place of the cashews. Use coconut or pumpkin seeds instead of sunflower seeds. Or try different kinds of dried fruit in place of the dates, such as dried apricots, apples, or dried prunes. The sky's the limit for possibilities! But please don't omit the sesame seeds or the wheat germ because that is what gives this recipe its special flavor.

HONEY BUTTER WHIP

½ cup butter (one cube)
½ cup honey
½ cup whipping cream

Let the butter stand at room temperature until softened. Gradually combine the honey, beating together until well blended. Add ½ cup whipping cream and beat with the electric mixer until light and fluffy. Serve with your favorite pancakes or waffles. If you want to make your pancake breakfast really, really special, serve HONEY BUTTER WHIP with fresh strawberries.

HONEY BUTTER

"Rouse yourself, my soul! Arise, O harp and lyre! Let us greet the dawn with song!" (Ps. 57:8 TLB).

½ cup butter (one cube)
½ cup honey

Let the butter stand at room temperature until softened. Gradually add an equal amount of honey, beating until the honey is well blended and the HONEY BUTTER is nice and fluffy. Serve with pancakes, waffles, or breakfast rolls.

HONEY CINNAMON TOAST

6 slices of bread, toasted
¼ cup butter or margarine, softened to
**   room temperature**
3 Tbsp. honey
½ tsp. cinnamon, or more according to taste

Lightly toast the six slices of bread in your toaster. While it's toasting stir the softened butter together with the honey and cinnamon. Spread on one side of the toast. Then grill under a preheated broiler in your oven for a few minutes, watching closely, until the edges start to bubble and brown. Serve immediately while piping hot.

MARILYN'S HOMEMADE GRANOLA

". . . weeping may endure for a night, but joy cometh in the morning" (Ps. 30:5).

Oven: 350°   Yield: 10 to 12 servings

½ cup honey

⅓ cup oil

½ tsp. vanilla

4 cups uncooked rolled oats

2 cups finely grated coconut (unsweetened)

1 cup walnuts or filberts, coarsely chopped

½ cup sesame seeds

¾ tsp. salt

3 tsp. cinnamon

In a small mixing bowl beat the honey together with the oil and vanilla until smooth and creamy. We use soy oil, but any mild vegetable oil will do, such as corn oil, safflower oil or one of the blends on the market today. Set the honey-oil mixture aside. Now in a large mixing bowl, stir together the oats, coconut, coarsely chopped nuts, sesame seeds, salt, and cinnamon. Pour the honey-oil mixture over the dry ingredients and mix well — first using a large wooden spoon and then mixing very thoroughly with your hands. Spread into two 9"x13" ungreased baking pans. Bake for about 25 minutes, stirring three or four times during the baking period. Watch closely and turn the oven temperature down to 300° if the granola starts turning a little too brown toward the end of the baking period. Store in an air-tight container. Serve with fresh fruit and milk. Homemade Granola is a delicious alternative to all the sugar coated crunchie breakfast cereal on the grocery shelves. Your family will love it too!

⅔ cup honey
2 lg. bananas

Measure the oil and honey into your blender. Process until smooth. Peel the bananas and slice them into the honey-oil mixture. Blend until smooth. Serve with sourdough pancakes, waffles or French toast.

FRESH BLUEBERRY TOPPING
1 cube butter or margarine
1 cup honey
1 cup fresh blueberries

Melt the butter in a small saucepan over low heat. Pour into a blender with the honey. Process until smooth. Add the fresh berries and blend again only until the berries are no longer whole. Serve immediately.

FRESH ORANGE TOPPING

Follow the same directions as with FRESH BLUEBERRY TOPPING, only use one large orange, peeled and quartered, plus a small piece of the orange peel. Process until the orange peel is blended in. Serve immediately with hot pancakes on plates that you have warmed.

FRESH STRAWBERRY TOPPING

Follow the same directions as with FRESH BLUEBERRY TOPPING, only use 1½ cups of fresh strawberries. Any other type of berries will work too, such as loganberries, marionberries, blackberries or raspberries.

FRESH FRUIT TOPPINGS
"The fruit of the righteous is a tree of life..."
(Prov. 11:30).

FRESH BANANA TOPPING
⅓ cup vegetable oil

A drop of honey catches more
flies than a barrel of vinegar.

Feed a man vinegar & you'll
eat no honey from his lips.

Every bee's honey is sweet.

George Herbert, Jacula Prudentum

TRAILSIDE BREAKFAST (APPLE MUESLI)

"Why spend your money on foodstuffs that don't give you strength? Why pay for groceries that don't do you any good?" (Isa. 55:2 TLB).

Yield: 2 servings

3 Tbsp. uncooked oatmeal
3 Tbsp. raisins
1 cup cold water
3 Tbsp. chopped walnuts
2 Tbsp. lemon juice
2 Tbsp. honey
1 lg. apple, unpeeled

Soak the oatmeal and raisins overnight in about one cup of cold water. The next morning, drain the water off and throw it away. Stir in the chopped walnuts with the softened oatmeal and raisins. Add the lemon and honey which you have stirred together until well blended. (For on the trail, you might like to have this blended ahead of time and packed along in a little plastic jar.) Wash the apple but do not peel. Grate it into the Muesli. Stir until evenly mixed. Serve with a cup of hot coffee and a piece of whole wheat bread (toasted, if you have the conveniences of home).

Muesli is an old breakfast idea that originated in Switzerland. It has many variations, but all of them are uncooked. You can vary the recipe by adding wheat germ, sunflower seeds, yogurt, or different kinds of nuts and dried fruit. Muesli is a wholesome, satisfying breakfast that sticks with you. And it's lower in calories than many breakfasts, too!

1 tsp. salt

⅓ cup vegetable oil

2 lg. eggs

1 tsp. baking soda dissolved in

1 tsp. water

The evening before you want SOURDOUGH PAN-CAKES for breakfast, take your starter out of the refrigerator. Add flour and water, about twice as much flour as water. But don't fill the sourdough crock up all the way to the top, or else it will work its way out during the night and you'll have a mess to clean up the next morning! Leave a couple of inches of working room for the starter. The starter should be set in a warm place overnight, covered.

In the morning stir together one cup of the sourdough starter with the powdered milk, salt, oil, and eggs. Last of all dissolve the baking soda in a teaspoonful of water and add it to the batter. Fry on a hot, greased griddle. Serve on warmed plates with one of the fresh fruit toppings or maybe with HONEY MAPLE SYRUP.

SOURDOUGH PANCAKES

"... I am come that they might have life, and that they might have it more abundantly" (John 10:10).

Yield: about 10 pancakes

1 cup thick sourdough starter

¼ cup dry powdered milk

HONEY MAPLE SYRUP

½ cup pure maple syrup

1 cup mild honey

2 Tbsp. butter

Stir together in a small saucepan and warm over low heat. Delicious with pancakes, waffles or French toast.

HOT HONEYED GRAPEFRUIT

" . . . But when you consider the wonderful truth of the prophets' words, then the light will dawn in your souls and Christ the Morning Star will shine in your hearts" (II Pet. 1.19 TLB).

Oven: 300°   Yield: 4 servings

2 grapefruit
¼ cup honey
¼ cup orange juice

Cut the grapefruit in half. Remove the seeds and the center. Then cut around each section with a grapefruit knife, freeing the fruit from the membranes. Blend the honey and orange juice thoroughly together, either by vigorous stirring in a small bowl or else use your blender. Trickle the honey-orange juice mixture over the top of each grapefruit half. Bake for about 15 minutes. Garnish with a red ripe strawberry or a maraschino cherry if desired. HOT HONEYED GRAPEFRUIT is great for a chilly, winter breakfast, It can also be served as a dessert or an appetizer before a special meal.

Tell me what you eat and I'll tell
you what you are.
Anthelme Brillat-Savarin,
Physiolgie du Gout

POPPYSEED HONEY TOAST

"Cause me to hear Your lovingkindness in the morning: for on You do I lean and in You do I trust. Cause me to know the way wherein I should walk, for I lift up my inner self to You" (Ps. 143:8 TAB).

6 slices of bread, toasted
¼ cup butter or margarine, softened to
       room temperature
2 Tbsp. honey
2 tsp. poppyseeds

Lightly toast the six slices of bread in your toaster. While they're toasting, stir the softened butter together with the honey and poppyseeds. Spread on one side of the toast. Then grill under a preheated broiler for a few minutes, watching closely, until the edges start to bubble and brown. Serve immediately! Delicious when served piping hot.

Beverages

ORANGE JULIE

"And Jesus arose, and rebuked the wind, and said unto the sea 'Peace be still.' And the wind ceased, and there was a great calm" (Mark 4:39).

Yield: 4 glasses

1 sm. can frozen orange juice (6 oz.)
1 cup milk
1 cup cold water
⅓ cup honey
1 tsp. vanilla
1 cup crushed ice

Put everything in the blender except the honey and mix for about 30 seconds. Drizzle in the honey and mix again, only until blended. If you don't have an ice crusher here's an easy way to make crushed ice: just stitch up an ice bag out of some sturdy blue jeans fabric — put the ice inside, and go to work with your hammer!

CITRUS SPARKLE

Yield: about 1 quart

¾ cup water
½ cup honey
2 oranges, peeled and quartered
½ lemon, peeled and quartered
2 limes, peeled and quartered
1 cup cubed pineapple
1 bottle 7 UP

Combine the water and honey in your blender. Add oranges, lemon, limes and pineapple. Cover and process again until the fruit is liquified. Pour each glass about half-full, add a few ice cubes and fill with 7 Up. This drink is a real thirst quencher!

Therefore doth heaven divide
The state of man in divers functions,
Setting endeavour in continual motion;
To which is fixed, as an aim or butt,
Obedience; for so work the honey-bees,
Creatures that by a rule in nature teach
The act of order to a peopled kingdom.

William Shakespeare
(1564-1616)
from King Henry V.

STRAWBERRY SMOOTHIE

Yield: 4 glasses

1 cup plain yogurt
1 cup cold milk
1 cup strawberries, stemmed and sliced
½ cup honey
1 tsp. lemon juice
1 cup crushed ice

Put all of the ingredients into your blender. Put the lid on, then blend until smooth. Serve immediately. This is a drink that you can be very imaginative with: use any fresh fruit that is in season — blackberries, raspberries, blueberries, to name a few.

DEEP SLEEP TEA

"I will both lay me down in peace, and sleep: for thou, Lord, only makest me dwell in safety" (Ps. 4:8).

Yield: 2 mugs

1 tsp. dried chamomile
2 cups boiling water
2 tsp. honey

Stir the dried chamomile into a small sauce pan of two cups of boiling water. Remove from heat and allow to seep for at least 5 minutes, with the lid on. Pour through a strainer into mugs. Sweeten each mug with a teaspoonful of honey. Deep Sleep chamomile tea will be enjoyed by young and old alike, especially at bedtime.

SLUSH PUNCH

"I will greatly rejoice in the Lord, my soul shall be joyful in my God; for He hath clothed me with the garments of salvation, He hath covered me with the robe of righteousness, as a bridegroom decketh himself with ornaments, and as a bride adorneth herself with her jewels" (Is. 61:10).

Yield: 1 gallon

12 oz. frozen orange juice concentrate
1 cup pineapple juice
Juice of 3 lemons
10 cups cold water
⅔ cup honey
2 bananas
1 cup frozen strawberries (partially thawed)

Mix the punch in a gallon jar or any other gallon capacity container. Stir the frozen orange juice together with the pineapple juice and the freshly squeezed lemon juice and the cold water, stirring until mixed. Take about one cupful of this juice that you have mixed and place it in your blender along with the two bananas which you have sliced and the honey. Process until the bananas are smoothly pureed. Add the bananas to the fruit punch. Now take about one more cupful of the juice and place it in the blender again, but this time with the partially frozen strawberries. Process until the strawberries are smoothly pureed. Stir the strawberries in with the fruit punch. Freeze at least 24 hours in airtight moisture proof container or containers. Remove from the freezer several hours before serving. It should be semi-frozen and thick to be good. Add carbonated beverage just before serving if desired. Stir and serve in the slush stage. Ideal for the holidays or any festive occasion.

SPICED TEA SPECIAL

Yield: about 8 servings

6 cups boiling water
6 tea bags
6 Tbsp. honey
1 stick of cinnamon
½ cup fresh lemon juice

Add the tea bags to the boiling water in a saucepan. Remove from heat and allow the tea to steep for five minutes with the lid on. Remove the tea bags. Place over low heat and stir in the honey. Add the cinnamon stick and lemon juice. Simmer slowly for 5 minutes. Serve in tea cups garnished with a little slice of lemon. Refrigerate any left over spiced tea. Later you can either warm it up again or else serve it as iced tea.

A swarm of bees in May
Is worth a load of hay;
A swarm of bees in June
Is worth a silver spoon;
A swarm of bees in July
Is not worth a fly.

Old English saying

ENERGY DRINK

"In a race, everyone runs but only one person gets first prize. So run your race to win" (1 Cor. 9:24 TLB).

Yield: 2 large glasses

¼ cup honey
½ cup unsweetened pineapple juice
1 banana, sliced
1 egg
1 cup cold milk
1 Tbsp. bee pollen

Put all the ingredients together in a blender and process until frothy. A great drink for joggers!

EGGNOG

"Beloved, I wish above all things that thou mayest prosper and be in health, even as thy soul prospereth" (3 John 2).

Yield: about 1 quart

3 cups milk
3 eggs
3 Tbsp. honey
½ tsp. pure vanilla extract
Dash of salt
1 cup crushed ice

Put all the ingredients except the ice into your blender and process until smooth. Next add the ice and process again until smooth. Serve immediately.

HONEYED CHOCOLATE

2 Tbsp. cocoa (or carob powder)
½ tsp. salt
3 Tbsp. honey
2 cups milk, scalded

Blend the cocoa (or carob powder) with the salt and honey. Add to the scalded milk and simmer over low heat for 2 or 3 minutes. Serve either hot or cold. If serving cold just pour over crushed ice in tall glasses.

CAROB-MINT SMOOTHIE

"You have made known to Me the ways of life: You will enrapture Me — diffusing My soul with joy — with and in Your presence" (Acts 2:28 TAB).

Yield: 2 tall glasses

4 tsp. carob powder (or cocoa)
¼ cup powdered milk
1 cup cold milk
Dash of salt
2 Tbsp. honey
1 cup crushed ice
2 drops mint oil

Mix all the ingredients together in your blender until smooth. Pour into tall glasses and serve immediately. Garnish with mint leaves if desired.

LEMONADE (HOT OR COLD)

"But you, beloved, build yourselves up [founded] on your most holy faith — make progress, rise like an edifice higher and higher — praying in the Holy Spirit" (Jude 20 TAB).

Yield: 2 servings

Juice of ½ lemon
1 cup water (hot or cold)
2 Tbsp. honey

Mix together the honey with the lemon juice and water. Just stir and serve. This is a very refreshing drink. If serving cold you might like to try adding HONEY ICE CUBES.

HONEY ICE CUBES

½ cup honey
2 cups very hot water
2 Tbsp. lemon juice

Blend the honey with the hot water and lemon juice. Pour into ice cube trays and freeze at once. Serve with lemonade or any fruit punch. Delicious in iced tea, too. "Cool it" with HONEY ICE CUBES.

NIGHTCAPS FOR TWO

Yield: 2 mugs

1⅓ cups milk
2 Tbsp. dried milk
1 Tbsp. honey
1 tsp. molasses
1 Tbsp. Bee Pollen
2 Tbsp. hot tap water

Warm the milk in a small sauce pan over low heat. Stir in the powdered dry milk, honey and molasses. Dissolve the Bee Pollen in 2 tablespoons of hot tap water and add to the milk. Pour in mugs and sip slowly.

Breads

CRACKED WHEAT BREAD

"And Jesus said unto them, I am the bread of life: he that cometh to me shall never hunger; and he that believeth on me shall never thirst" (John 6:35).

Oven: 350°   Yield: 4 large loaves

2 cups cracked wheat
¼ cup oatmeal (dry)
¼ cup dry instant mashed potatoes
¼ cup cornmeal
6 cups water
¼ cup molasses
¼ cup honey
½ cup vegetable oil
1 Tbsp. salt
1½ cups dry milk
4 eggs (slightly beaten)
2 Tbsp. yeast
½ cup warm water
1 tsp. honey
¼ tsp. ginger
2 cups whole wheat flour
10 to 11 cups white flour

In a large, heavy saucepan stir together the following ingredients with 6 cups of warm water: the cracked wheat, oatmeal, instant potatoes, and cornmeal. Cook together over medium-low heat for 20 minutes, stirring occasionally. Remove from stove and cool. When cooled to lukewarm add the molasses, honey, oil, salt, dry milk, and slightly beaten eggs. Mix thoroughly with wooden spoon. In a small bowl dissolve the yeast in ½ cup warm water with 1 teaspoon honey and ¼ teaspoon ginger. When it's nice and bubbly, add to the other mixture, stirring vigorously. Next stir in the whole wheat flour. Gradually add 10-11 cups of white flour, stirring and mixing well till the dough no longer clings to the sides of the bowl. Turn out on a floured bread board and knead for a good 10 minutes. (You'll love the feeling of "life" in this dough!) Place in greased bowl (turning to grease the top), and let rise in a warm place till doubled — about one hour. Turn out on an oiled bread board and divide the dough in fourths. Let rest for 10 minutes before shaping into loaves. Place in greased, large loaf pans (9⅝" x 5½") and return to warm place till nearly doubled again, about an hour. Place in preheated oven and bake for 45 to 50 minutes till done. Remove from pans and cool on wire racks. You'll agree that this is a truly superb bread — well worth the extra effort!

Even bees, the little almsmen of spring bowers,
Know there is richest juice in poison-flowers.

John Keats, Isabella

BRAN MUFFINS

"Oh, that we might know the Lord! Let us press on to know Him, and He will respond to us as surely as the coming of dawn or the rain of early spring" (Hos. 6:3 TLB).

Oven: 350°   Yield: 6 muffins

1 cup whole wheat flour
½ cup unprocessed miller's bran
½ tsp. baking soda
1½ Tbsp. honey
¼ tsp. salt
1 cup plain yogurt

Measure out the flour, bran, and soda into a mixing bowl. Stir together with a fork until the mixture is well distributed. If you're fixing these for breakfast, you might like to do this much the night before. Now in a separate little bowl stir together the yogurt, honey and salt. Carefully stir into the flour mixture until all the flour is mixed. Spoon out the batter into your well-greased muffin tins and bake in a preheated oven for about 30 minutes. Serve warm with butter and of course, "Please pass the HONEY!"

36   BREADS

APPLESAUCE NUT BREAD

"How beautiful upon the mountains are the feet of those who bring the happy news of peace and salvation . . ." (Isa. 52:7 TLB).

Oven: 350°   Yield: 1 large loaf

1 cup white flour
2 cups whole wheat flour
1 tsp. baking powder
2 tsp. baking soda
1 tsp. salt
½ tsp. cinnamon
2 cups chopped walnuts
1¼ cups applesauce
⅔ cup honey
2 Tbsp. salad oil
¼ cup orange juice
1 egg, beaten

Measure all the dry ingredients and the chopped nuts together in a large mixing bowl and toss to mix. Make a well in the dry ingredients and add the applesauce, honey, salad oil, orange juice and beaten egg which you have previously beat together with your electric mixer. Stir rapidly into the dry ingredients, using a fold over motion. Do not beat or stir too long. As with any quick bread, stir only until all the dry ingredients are moistened. Empty the batter into a large greased loaf pan (9⅝"x5½"). Bake for about 60 minutes or until bread is done.

JOYCE'S SURPRISE SANDWICH BREAD

"For where your treasure is, there will your heart be also" (Matt. 6:21).

Oven: 350°   Yield: 2 medium loaves

1 Tbsp. dry yeast
1¼ cup warm water
1 Tbsp. honey
1½ tsp. salt
⅛ tsp. ginger
3½ cups white flour
1½ cups very thinly sliced wieners
1½ cups finely diced cheddar cheese
1 cup raisins
¼ cup well-drained pickle relish

Stir yeast into the warm water in a small bowl and let stand 5 minutes to soften. Add the honey, salt, and ginger and stir until dissolved. Measure out 2 cups of flour in a medium-sized bowl. Pour in the yeast mixture and beat at high speed for 2 minutes. Now stir in the remaining 1½ cups of flour by hand and mix thoroughly. Turn out on a floured bread board and knead until dough is elastic (takes about 5 minutes). Place dough in a greased bowl. Cover with a dish towel, and let rise in a warm place till double (about 1 hour). While the dough is rising prepare the wiener slices, the diced cheese, the raisins and drain the pickle relish. Mix all four ingredients together in a bowl and set aside. When the bread dough has doubled, turn it out on a bread board and cut in 2 equal pieces. With oiled hands shape each piece into a flat rectangle (about 8"x11"). Now divide the wiener mixture evenly and spread on the dough up to about 2" from the edge. Turn up all the edges of the dough, sealing the "goodies" inside. Now carefully knead to evenly distribute all the ingredients. Shape in loaves and place in 2 greased 8½"x4½" pans. Cover, and let rise until double (about an hour) in a warm place. Bake in preheated oven for 50 minutes until crusty brown. Cool on rack. Now you have a built-in sandwich; perfect for lunches. Who isn't ready for a little variety in the "brown bag"?

BANANA BREAD

"... Know ye not that a little leaven leaveneth the whole lump?" (1 Cor. 5:6).

Oven: 325°   Yield: 1 large loaf

1 cup white flour
1¼ cups whole wheat flour
½ tsp. salt
1 tsp. baking soda
½ cup butter
¾ cup honey
2 eggs, beaten
1 cup mashed ripe bananas (about 3)
2-3 Tbsp. hot water
½ cup chopped walnuts

In a medium bowl, stir together the white flour, whole wheat flour, salt, and soda. Set aside. In a large heavy saucepan on low heat, melt the butter. Stir in the honey with the butter and remove from heat. Add the beaten eggs and the mashed banana and stir vigorously, combining thoroughly. Carefully stir in about half of the dry ingredients, then half the hot water. Now add the rest of the dry ingredients, then the rest of the hot water, making a light, smooth dough. Last of all, stir in the nuts. Fill a greased and floured loaf-pan (9⅝"x5½"), and bake for 70 minutes or until brown and starting to pull away from the edge of the pan. Cool in the pan on a rack. Turn out and wrap well when completely cooled. Store a day in the refrigerator before slicing. You'll love this delicious version of the all-time, favorite banana bread. Good in lunches, snacks, or even as a dessert — as is!

CREAM 'N HONEY WHEAT BREAD

"Great peace have they which love thy law: and nothing shall offend them" (Ps. 119:165).

Oven: 375°   Yield: 4 medium loaves

2 cups very hot water
⅔ cup honey
2 cups heavy sweet cream
2 Tbsp. salt
4 Tbsp. yeast
8 lg. eggs (room temperature)
12 to 13 cups whole wheat flour

Dissolve the honey in water and add the cream. When the mixture is warm, stir in the yeast. Then add 4 cups of whole wheat flour and mix well with an electric mixer for 5 minutes. Add the eggs which have been previously set out of the refrigerator to warm to room temperature. Mix well. Now add the rest of the flour, gradually stirring in with a wooden spoon. Turn out on a well floured bread board and knead until smooth. Add a little more flour as needed during the kneading process. This bread will, by nature, be a little more sticky than most — it's supposed to be that way. Place the dough in a large bowl that you have generously oiled with vegetable oil, turning to oil the top side. Place the dough in a warm place to rise until doubled in size. At the warm setting on the oven (100°), it will take about 45 minutes. Turn out the dough on an oiled surface and cut into four equal pieces with an oiled bread knife. Shape in loaves and place in greased medium sized loaf pans (8½"x4½"). Return to warm place and let dough rise again for about 30 minutes. Do not allow this dough to rise as much as ordinary bread because you'll find it will rise more as it's being baked. Bake in preheated oven for about 40 minutes. Remove from pans immediately and cool on wire racks. This is also a fine basic recipe to use for buns or sweet rolls.

I never had a piece of toast
Particularly long and wide,
But fell upon the sanded floor,
And always on the buttered side.

James Payn, Chamber's Journal. 1884

SOURDOUGH

"Lord, thou hast been our dwelling place in all generations. Before the mountains were brought forth, or ever thou hadst formed the earth and the world, even from everlasting to everlasting, thou art God" (Ps. 90:1, 2).

The oldtimers in the Alaskan wilderness carried a little crock of yeasty sourdough starter with them. From this starter, they would mix up their traditionally tangy pancakes or bread. The sourdough starter was kept "alive" year after year. Each time a little was used from the crock, a little more flour and water would be added, and the starter would continue to "work." Some of you may be fortunate to have a sourdough starter that originated with the oldtimers in Alaska. In their tradition of hospitality, the sourdough was often divided and the precious starter shared with a friend. Because of its history and tradition, sourdough cookery has a certain nostalgia — a certain hearty homemade quality. You will enjoy all of the sourdough recipes included in **JOY WITH HONEY.** The three I have included are SOURDOUGH PANCAKES, GRANDMA'S LITTLE HONEY BUNS, and SOURDOUGH CAROB CAKE.

The best way to start your own sourdough pot is to find someone who will share his "starter" with you. But if there doesn't happen to be a sourdough baker among your friends, you can start one in your own kitchen. Mix together in a crock or cookie jar:

2 cups flour
½ tsp. dry yeast dissolved in
1½ cups lukewarm water
1 tsp. salt
3 Tbsp. sugar

Keep the crock covered and allow it to sit for two or three days in a fairly warm place. Stir once or twice daily. Now you have your starter. It should be kept in the refrigerator and taken out the night before you want to use from it. Since you never want to use up all the starter, you must always add flour and water to it the night before you use it. Add about twice as much flour as water. You can use either white or wholewheat flour, but wholewheat is especially good with pancakes. Don't fill the crock too full when mixing the flour and water the night before, or the next morning you'll find it has worked its way right out of the crock and all over your cabinet! You should use your starter at least once every two weeks.

"A+" SOURDOUGH BREAD

This recipe consistently turns out beautifully textured, uniform loaves every time we bake it. That's why it deserves an "A+!"

Oven: 350°   Yield: 4 large loaves

**Four days before you want to bake, mix your starter:
SOURDOUGH STARTER (step 1)**

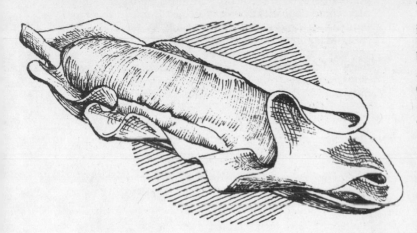

SOURDOUGH SPONGE (step 2)

The evening before you make bread, mix the following and cover overnight. This is called the "sponge." Keep it at room temperature, in your largest mixing bowl.

All of the starter
6 cups white flour
1 cup honey
4 cups warm water

SOURDOUGH BREAD (step 3)

The next morning when the sponge is nice and bubbly make your "A+" sourdough bread. Mix the following together:

All of the sponge
1 tsp. ginger dissolved in 4 tsp. warm water
¼ cup honey
1 Tbsp. salt
½ cup oil
10-12 cups flour (2 or 3 cups can be whole wheat
   if desired)

Mix together and knead until smooth and elastic. You'll love the feeling of life in this dough as you knead it. Place in greased bowl and let rise in a warm place until double in size. Turn out onto an oiled bread board and divide into 4 equal pieces. Form into loaves and place in large 9⅝"x5½" pans. Let rise again until almost doubled. Bake for 45 minutes. Share generously.

2 cups warm water
2 cups white flour
1 Tbsp. yeast
1 Tbsp. salt
1 Tbsp. honey

Dissolve yeast in ½ cup of the warm water. Let set for 5 minutes. Add remaining ingredients. Put in a crock or bowl and cover for 4 days, stirring once daily. It will smell quite yeasty and separate — that's just fine! If your plans get changed on day 4, never fear; you can put the starter in the refrigerator, but warm to room temperature when ready to use.

CRANBERRY HONEY LOAF

"Go thy way, eat thy bread with joy . . . " (Eccles. 9:7).

Oven: 350°   Yield: 1 loaf

2 cups white flour
1 tsp. baking powder
1½ tsp. baking soda
1 egg
¼ cup margarine
1 tsp. salt
1 Tbsp. grated orange rind
⅔ cup honey
⅔ cup orange juice
½ cup chopped walnuts
1 cup raw cranberries

Stir the flour, baking powder and baking soda together in a mixing bowl and set aside. In another bowl mix the egg, softened margarine, salt, and honey, beating until well blended. Pour in the orange juice slowly and continue beating. Chop up the raw cranberries — (your blender will do a beautiful job of this on low speed). Add the chopped cranberries and the chopped nuts to the honey mixture and stir until blended. Add the dry ingredients last of all, stirring only until the flour is all mixed in. The secret of success with this bread, as with all quick breads, is not to stir the batter too much after adding the dry ingredients. Spoon carefully into a greased loaf pan (8½"x4½"). Bake in a preheated oven for 50 to 60 minutes or until a toothpick comes out clean when testing. Remove from pan immediately and cool on a wire rack. When completely cool, wrap in a plastic bag or foil and place in the refrigerator. The flavors will blend together with one or two days' aging. Or you might like to make this festive Cranberry Honey Loaf up a few weeks before the busy holiday season. It also freezes very well.

BAGELS

"Behold, God is my salvation; I will trust and not be afraid; for the Lord Jehovah is my strength and my song; He also is become my salvation" (Isa. 12:2).

Oven: 375°   Yield: 12 bagels

2 cups whole wheat flour
2 cups white flour
3 Tbsp. honey
1 Tbsp. salt
2 Tbsp. yeast
1½ cups very hot tap water
1 egg white (beaten)
1 Tbsp. cold water

In a large mixing bowl combine 1½ cups of whole wheat flour with the salt and undissolved active dry yeast. Stir in the honey with the very hot tap water and then add gradually to the dry ingredients; beat at medium speed for 2 minutes, scraping bowl occasionally. Add remaining ½ cup of whole wheat flour and beat at high speed with electric mixer for 2 more minutes. Stir in the white flour gradually — enough to make a soft dough. Turn out on a lightly floured board and knead for about 10 minutes until the dough is smooth and elastic. Place in an ungreased bowl, cover; let rise in a warm place for 20 minutes. Turn out onto a lightly floured board and press into a circle about 12" in diameter. With a nice sharp knife cut the dough into 12 pie shape pieces. Roll up each piece, small end first, and shape into a smooth ball. Punch a hole in the center of each with a floured finger. Pull gently to enlarge hole, working each bagel into uniform shape (looks similar to a doughnut). Place on ungreased baking sheets, leaving about an inch space between each bagel. Cover, first with a piece of plastic wrap and then a light towel; let rise in a warm place for about 20 minutes. Fill a large pan with a gallon of hot water sweetened with 1 tablespoon of honey. Bring to a boil; lower heat and add four bagels at a time. Simmer for 7 minutes, turning once after the first 3 minutes. Remove from water and place on paper towels to drain and cool for 5 minutes. Place on ungreased baking sheets. Bake in a preheated oven for 10 minutes. Remove from oven and brush with the egg whites and water. (The water is stirred into the foamy egg whites after beating them.) Return to oven, bake about 20 minutes longer or until done. They should be golden brown. Remove from baking sheets immediately and cool on wire racks. To make a sandwich, split bagel and spread with softened cream cheese. Add a little smoked salmon if desired.

Full merrily the humble-bee doth sing,
Till he hath lost his honey and his sting;
And being once subdued in armed tail,
Sweet honey and sweet notes together fail.

Shakespeare, Troilus and Cressida

HAMBURGER BUNS

"Fix your thoughts on what is true and right. Think about things that are pure and lovely, and dwell on the fine, good things in others. Think about all you can praise God for and be glad about" (Phil. 4:8 TLB).

Oven: 400°   Yield: 12 buns

1 cup whole wheat flour

5 cups white flour

1½ tsp. salt

2 Tbsp. yeast

2 Tbsp. soft butter

3 Tbsp. honey

2 cups hot tap water

Mix the whole wheat flour and one cup of the white flour together in a large bowl, and stir together with the dry yeast and salt. In a small bowl stir the honey into two cups of very hot tap water. Add the hot water-honey mixture to the dry ingredients gradually, stirring all the time. Stir in the butter. Beat for two minutes at medium speed with your electric mixer. Stir in one more cup of white flour, to make a thicker batter and beat for another two minutes; this time at high speed. Stir in 2½ more cups of white flour or enough to make a stiff dough that doesn't cling to the sides of the bowl. Turn out onto a floured bread board and knead until smooth and elastic. Place in a greased bowl, turning to grease the top. Cover, and let rise in a warm place till double in size (about 30 minutes). Punch the dough down and place on an oiled surface. With an oiled knife cut the dough in 12 equal pieces. Shape each piece into a smooth ball. You may want to use a little oil on your hands, too, if the dough sticks. Place the balls of dough on two greased cookie sheets, leaving at least 2" of space between each, as they will continue to rise more. Place in a warm spot and allow them to rise for another 30 minutes or until doubled. Bake for 15 to 20 minutes or until done. Remove from cookie sheets immediately and cool on wire racks. Cover with a light towel if you would like the crust to soften up a little. If desired, you can sprinkle ¼ teaspoon sesame seeds on the top of each ball of dough before the last rising. The All-American hamburger was never better!

Bees work for man, and yet they never bruise
Their Master's flower, but leave it, having done,
As fair as ever and as fit to use;
So both the flower doth stay, and honey run.

George Herbert, Providence

44   BREADS

HONEY-DILL BATTER BREAD

"The entrance and unfolding of Your words gives light; it gives understanding — discernment and comprehension — to the simple" (Ps. 119:130 TAB).

Oven: 350°   Yield: 1 loaf

1 Tbsp. yeast
¼ cup warm water
1 cup creamed cottage cheese
2 Tbsp. honey
1 Tbsp. instant minced onion
1 Tbsp. butter
2 tsp. dill seed
1 tsp. salt
¼ tsp. baking soda
1 egg
1 cup whole wheat flour
1½ cups white flour

Dissolve the yeast in the warm water. Set aside. In a sauce pan heat the cottage cheese to just lukewarm. Now add the honey, dried onion, butter, dill seed, salt, baking soda and egg in a bowl and mix thoroughly with the cottage cheese and yeast. Stir in the whole wheat flour, beating well. Now stir in the white flour and mix thoroughly to form a stiff dough. Cover with a dish towel and place in warm spot. Allow the dough to double in bulk (takes from 45 to 50 minutes in a warm 100° oven). Stir down the dough. Turn into a well greased, medium sized loaf pan (8½"x4½"). Return dough to warm spot and let rise for another 30 minutes till it is light. Bake for 40 to 50 minutes, or until brown. Brush with melted butter when it comes out of the oven and then sprinkle with a little salt. For a real homey idea try baking this bread in a round 8-inch casserole dish.

ZUCCHINI BREAD

"Blessed . . . are those who dwell in Your house and Your presence; they will be singing Your praises all the day long" (Ps. 84:4 TAB).

Oven: 350°   Yield: 3 small loaves

1 cup honey
1 cup oil
2 eggs
1 tsp. baking soda
1 tsp. salt
1 tsp. baking powder
1 tsp. cinnamon

2½ cups shredded zucchini
1 cup whole wheat flour
2½ cups white flour
1 tsp. vanilla
½ cup chopped walnuts

Mix the honey, oil and eggs in a mixing bowl. In a separate bowl stir all the dry ingredients together. Add to the honey mixture, alternating with the shredded zucchini. Last of all stir in the vanilla. Divide the batter equally between three small loaf pans that have already been greased and lightly floured. Bake for 45 minutes to 1 hour. Check for doneness with toothpick inserted in center. It should come out clean.

WHOLE WHEAT POTATO BREAD

"From the rising of the sun unto the going down of the same the Lord's name is to be praised" (Ps. 113:3).

Oven: 350°   Yield: 4 medium loaves

2 Tbsp. yeast
5 cups warm water (110°-115°)
6 Tbsp. oil
¼ cup honey
4 cups whole wheat flour
1 cup mashed potatoes
½ cup dry milk
1 Tbsp. salt
7 to 8 cups white flour

Sprinkle the yeast in ½ cup of warm water and stir to dissolve. Set aside. In a large pan stir together the oil and honey over low heat till well mixed and slightly warm. Remove from stove and add the mashed potatoes and the remaining 4½ cups of warm water, beating until well mixed. In a separate bowl measure out the whole wheat flour, dry milk and salt. Stir the dry ingredients together; then add to the mixture in the saucepan, beating until smooth. Now add the yeast mixture and beat to blend. Then with a wooden spoon gradually stir in the white flour. When the dough no longer sticks to the sides of the bowl you have enough flour. Now turn out onto a lightly floured bread board and knead for about 10 minutes. The dough will be smooth and satiny. Then grease the bowl and place the dough in it; turning over to grease the top. Cover with a dish towel and let rise in a warm place (80° to 100°) for 1 to 1½ hours. Punch down dough, turn onto board and divide into four equal pieces. Cover and let rest for 5 minutes. Shape into four loaves and place in greased 8½"x4½" loaf pans. Cover and return to warm place to rise again until doubled, about 1 hour. Bake for 45 to 50 minutes. To test for doneness remove one of the loaves from the pan by lightly tapping on the bottom of the pan. Then tap again on the bottom of the loaf. If you hear a hollow sound the bread is done. Otherwise return the loaf to the oven for another 5 minutes. Another sign of doneness is when the bread pulls away from the sides of the pan. When you are sure the bread is done, remove from loaf pans and let cool on a wire rack. You may wish to brush the tops of the loaves with soft butter. We do!

Be gentle
    When you touch bread.
        Let it not be
            uncared for, unwanted.
                So often bread
                    Is taken for granted.
There is so much beauty
    in bread —
Beauty of sun and soil,
Beauty of patient toil.
Winds and rains have caressed it,
    Christ often blessed it.
Be gentle
    When you touch bread.
                    author unknown

While Honey lies in Every Flower, no doubt,
It takes a Bee to get the Honey out.

Arthur Guiterman, A Poet's Proverbs.

HONEY-ORANGE RYE BREAD

"Pleasant words are as an honeycomb, sweet to the soul, and health to the bones" (Prov. 16:24).

Oven: 375°   Yield: 4 medium loaves

2 Tbsp. dry yeast
½ cup warm water
½ cup honey
½ cup molasses
2 Tbsp. salt
½ cup vegetable oil
3 cups hot water
3 cups rye flour
¼ cup grated orange peel
8 to 9 cups white flour

Soften the yeast in ½ cup of warm water. In a large bowl, mix together honey, molasses, salt, and oil. Stir in 3 cups hot water. Stir in the rye flour, then beat well. Now add the softened yeast and the orange peel; mix well. Stir in enough flour to make soft dough. Cover with a dish towel and let rest for 10 minutes. Turn out the dough on a well floured bread board and knead for 10 minutes. Place dough in a lightly greased bowl, turning once to grease surface. Cover and let rise in a warm place till doubled (about 1½ hours). Punch down. Turn out on lightly floured board and divide in four equal portions. Shape each into smooth ball. Cover and let rest for 10 minutes. Now shape in four loaves and place in greased, medium-sized (8½"x4½") pans. Cover and return to warm place to rise till double (about 1 hour). Bake in preheated oven for about 30 minutes. For a softer crust, brush with soft margarine or butter. Cool on rack, if you can wait that long. Warm bread is such a treat. Plan it to come out of the oven just as the children come home from school or a pleasant surprise for hubby. It will slice warm beautifully with an electric slicing knife, or a very sharp bread knife.

PEANUT BREAD

"Better is a dry morsel with quietness than a house full of feasting (on offered sacrifices) with strife (Prov. 17:1 TAB).

Oven: 350°   Yield: 1 loaf

3 Tbsp. dry yeast
1 tsp. salt

½ cup dry powdered milk
½ tsp. ginger
1 cup hot water
½ cup honey
1 cup freshly coarse ground peanuts
2 cups whole wheat flour
2 cups white flour

In a medium-sized bowl stir together the yeast, salt, dry powdered milk and the ginger. In a small bowl stir together the honey and hot water. Now it should be just warm, so add to the yeast mixture and beat at high speed with your electric mixer for one minute. Then with a spoon stir in the peanuts which you have ground in a nut grinder. Continue with vigorous hand stirring, first adding the whole wheat flour, then stirring in the white flour until the dough is thoroughly mixed. Now turn out the dough on a very lightly floured board. No kneading! Just gently roll it back and forth shaping it into a loaf. Place in an oiled, medium-sized pan (8½"x4½"). Oil top and smooth with your fingers to even the surface. Let rise to the top of the pan in a warm place (about 2 hours). I find the oven set on warm is just right (about 100°). Be patient. This is a very heavy dough but the results are well worth the effort; a rich flavorful bread! Preheat oven and bake for about 45 minutes. Cool on a rack. Slice very thinly and top with honey if desired. It's delicious toasted too, for a hearty breakfast. Peanuts are rich in minerals, vitamins and protein. The children will love this bread.

SOURDOUGH ENGLISH MUFFINS

"But the good man walks along in the ever-brightening light of God's favor; the dawn gives way to morning splendor" (Prov. 6:18 TLB).

Griddle: 375°   Yield: ten 3" muffins

½ cup sourdough starter
1 cup milk
2 cups whole wheat flour
1 tsp. honey

Make one cup of warm milk with warm tap water and non-fat dry milk. In a bowl combine the warm milk with the starter, whole wheat flour and honey. Mix well and cover. Let it "work" on your countertop overnight or for about 8 hours. Yes, in the bowl please!

The next morning or 8 hours later add the following:

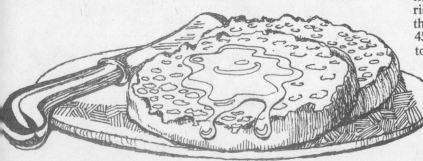

1 Tbsp. honey
½ cup white flour
¾ tsp. salt
½ tsp. soda

Drizzle the honey over the dough in the bowl. Stir the salt and soda together with the white flour, then sprinkle over the dough on top of the honey. Now thoroughly mix all the ingredients togther. Turn out the dough on a floured board and knead for 2 or 3 minutes until no longer sticky. Roll or pat out the dough to ¾" thickness and cut out 10 - 3" muffins. (An empty tuna fish can is just the right size). Dip the edge of the can in a little vegetable oil to prevent sticking. Place on waxed paper (over a cookie sheet) that has been sprinkled with about 2 Tbsp. of cornmeal. Allow a little space between the muffins as they will expand. Sprinkle a little cornmeal on top of each muffin, too. Cover well so they won't dry out during the rising time. (I use a piece of plastic wrap first and then a light towel). Let rise in a warm place for about 45 minutes. Bake on a lightly greased griddle for 8 to 10 minutes per side, turning once. When done, slice them in half horizontally and serve them with breakfast, lunch or dinner. Especially delicious when loaded with lots of butter and honey. If you have any leftovers pop them in the toaster; they'll be just as good as the fresh ones right off the griddle!

100% WHOLE WHEAT BREAD

"Man shall not live by bread alone, but by every word that proceedeth out of the mouth of God" (Matt. 4:4).

Oven: 350°   Yield: 4 medium loaves

10 to 12 cups home-ground whole wheat flour
4 Tbsp. dry yeast
2 cups powdered milk
4 cups warm water
1 cup honey
½ cup vegetable oil
2 Tbsp. salt

If you are fortunate enough to own a little flour grinder or an attachment on your mixer to grind flour, this is a recipe you'll love. The flour will be warm immediately after you have ground it. This is the big factor that adds to the success of this recipe. You can get similar good results by warming store-bought whole wheat flour in the oven at 100°. Of course, another advantage of the fresh ground flour is both better nutrition and irresistible flavor.

In a large mixing bowl, combine 6 cups of the whole wheat flour with the yeast and dry milk. Heat together water, honey, oil and salt just until warm (115° to 120°), stirring constantly. Check the temperature with a thermometer. Add to dry ingredients in mixing bowl. Beat at low speed of electric mixer for ½ minute, scraping sides of the bowl. Then beat for 3 minutes at high speed. By hand, stir in enough of the remaining whole wheat flour to make a soft dough. Turn out on a floured bread board and knead until smooth and elastic, about 5 minutes. Shape into a ball and place in a greased bowl, turning once to grease surface. Cover; let rise in warm place till almost double, about 30 minutes. Punch dough down. Cover and let rest 10 minutes. Divide dough into four equal portions and shape into loaves. Place in medium-sized bread pans (8½"x4½"). Cover; let rise till almost double in a warm place, about 20 minutes. Bake for 35 to 40 minutes. Remove from pan. Cool on wire rack. This bread freezes beautifully. Just make sure the loaves are completely cooled before wrapping them for the freezer.

BARLEY LOAVES

"There is a lad here, which hath five loaves, and two small fishes: but what are they among so many?" (John 6:9).

Oven: 350°   Yield: 4 medium loaves

1 cup pearl barley
3 cups water
½ cup warm water
1 tsp. honey
¼ tsp. ginger
2 Tbsp. dry yeast
2 cups warm water
¼ cup honey

2 cups whole wheat flour
½ cup soft butter
1 Tbsp. salt
6 cups enriched white flour

Simmer the barley in 3 cups water until it has absorbed all the water and is tender — about 45 minutes. Let cool until only warm before adding to the bread dough. Combine the honey, ginger, and yeast in ½ cup warm water and let stand in warm place until bubbling nicely. In a large bowl stir together 2 cups warm water, ¼ cup honey and 2 cups whole wheat flour. Add the yeast mixture and beat well. Add butter and salt. Add 4 cups white flour and the slightly warm, cooked barley. Stir until the dough clears the bowl. Spread the remaining 2 cups flour on the bread board, turn out the dough and knead vigorously, using more flour if necessary as the heaviness of the barley requires a fairly stiff dough to hold it in suspension as it bakes. Return to the greased bowl, cover and let rise in a warm place until double in bulk. Turn out on bread board, divide into 4 equal portions, shape into loaves and place in greased 8½"x4½" pans. Cover and return to warm place until light — approximately 20 minutes. This dough rises very quickly, so watch it closely. Bake for about 45 minutes. If desired, brush tops of loaves with butter about 5 minutes before the end of the baking period. Turn pans on sides and allow to cool for a few minutes before removing from pans. Warm bread slices beautifully with an electric slicing knife. What a treat!

GRANDMA'S LITTLE HONEY BUNS

"But He would feed you with the choicest foods. He would satisfy you with honey for the taking" (Ps. 81:16 TLB).

Oven: 375°   Yield: 3 dozen

6 cups flour
1 Tbsp. dry yeast
½ cup sourdough starter
2 cups lukewarm water (90°-95°)
2 Tbsp. real melted butter
1 scant Tbsp. salt
¼ cup honey
⅓ cup nonfat dry milk

These little honey buns are my mother's own recipe. In our family they have been a favorite for many years, especially at the happy holiday season.

Measure the flour into a large bowl (5-6 quart). Make a well in the flour and set in a warm place (85°-95°). Sprinkle dry yeast over the top of one cup of warm water and set aside in warm place. (Mother's secret warm spot is on the floor under the wood stove.) In the other cup of warm water stir in honey, salt, dry milk, melted butter, and sourdough starter; combine this with dissolved yeast. Gradually stir yeast mixture into the warmed flour. Knead until smooth and elastic. Add a little more water or flour if needed. Grease the bowl with a tablespoon of vegetable oil, and place the dough in it, turning once to oil the top. Cover with a light towel and put in a warm place again out of draft. When double in bulk (about 45 minutes) knead down and again cover and let rise for about 20 minutes in a warm place. Then knead down again and form into 1½-inch balls and place on greased cookie sheet about 2 inches apart. Oil the top as you place each bun on cookie sheet. Cover and put in warm place to rise. When double in bulk bake for 20-25 minutes. Turn out immediately on rack to cool. Cover with a light towel to soften the crust.

Salads & Dressings

WATERCRESS TOSSED SALAD

"They looked to Him, and were radiant..." (Ps. 34:5 TAB).

Yield: 6 to 8 servings

1 bunch watercress
1 head iceberg lettuce
2 lg. tomatoes, cut up
1 stalk celery, sliced
2 green onions, chopped

Wash the watercress thoroughly in a sinkful of cool water. Shake off excess water and wrap in a paper towel, then in a plastic bag. Place in the refrigerator for at least an hour to allow to crispen. Prepare the lettuce ahead of time in the same way. Chop the watercress, stems and all, into a large salad bowl. Tear apart the iceberg lettuce, breaking into bite-sized pieces with your fingers. Toss together with the watercress. Add the tomatoes, celery, and green onions; toss again. Serve immediately, accompanied with POPPY SEED DRESSING.

POPPY SEED DRESSING

½ cup mild honey
1 tsp. dry mustard
1 tsp. salt
⅓ cup apple cider vinegar
1 Tbsp. fresh onion puree
1 cup vegetable oil, soy oil preferred
1½ Tbsp. poppy seeds

Measure the honey, dry mustard, salt and apple cider vinegar directly into your blender or mixing bowl. Process until smooth. Make the fresh onion puree by rubbing a sweet onion over the finest part of your hand grater. Add to the dressing. Start the blender and gradually add the oil in a slow stream. Process until thoroughly blended. Stop the blender and sprinkle the poppy seeds on top. Flip the blender on and off three or four times until the seeds are mixed in. Place in a serving bowl and let the folks help themselves. Poppy seed dressing is a delicious accompaniment to any tossed green salad. It is also good served with avocados, grapefruit slices and apples on a crisp bed of romaine. Use your imagination.

LOUIS DRESSING

½ cup mayonnaise
¼ cup catsup
2 Tbsp. apple cider vinegar
1 tsp. honey
¼ cup sweet pickles, finely chopped
1 hard-boiled egg, finely chopped
Dash of salt

Mix well — either by hand or with an electric mixer, but **not** in a blender. Keep refrigerated until ready to serve.

CRAB LOUIS

"For the angel of the Lord guards and rescues all who reverence him" (Ps. 34:7 TLB).

Yield: 2 hearty servings

1 sm. head iceberg lettuce, broken in little pieces
2 leaves Romaine lettuce, torn in small pieces
2 green onions, chopped
½ cup slivers of red cabbage
6 radishes, in halves or rosettes
1 ripe avocado, sliced
2 tomatoes in wedges
2 hard-boiled eggs, halved
1 cucumber, cut in long strips
All the meat from one large crab

Toss the iceberg and Romaine together with the red cabbage and onions. Divide on two dinner plates. Arrange the radish rosettes, avocado slices, tomato wedges, hard-boiled eggs and cucumber strips. Last of all, pile the fresh crab meat on top. Serve with LOUIS DRESSING. This is a dinner in itself, and a very special one — deserving music and candlelight!

GARDEN GREEN SALAD

"And the Lord shall guide thee continually, and satisfy thy soul in drought, and make fat thy bones: and thou shalt be like a watered garden, and like a spring of water, whose waters fail not" (Isa. 58:11).

Yield: about 4 servings

Several leaves of fresh lettuce, washed and torn
1 or 2 leaves of fresh spinach, washed and torn
2 green onions, washed and chopped
1 small sized zucchini, washed and sliced
3 or 4 radishes, scrubbed and halved
2 or 3 sm. carrots, scrubbed and sliced
2 or 3 flowerettes of cauliflower, broken

Combine all the freshly "picked" and prepared vegetables together in a large bowl. Toss lightly. Serve with your favorite dressing. Our favorite is the following honey version of an ever popular French Dressing.

What a joy it is to have vegetables out of your own garden. If you aren't blessed with any land, you might like to consider growing a little vegetable garden in planter boxes on your patio or possibly a window box. Nothing beats your own home-grown vegetables. You'll be amazed at what just one little seed will do!

FRENCH DRESSING

Yield: ¾ cup

½ cup salad oil, chilled
2 Tbsp. apple cider vinegar
2 Tbsp. lemon juice
1 tsp. honey
½ tsp. salt
½ tsp. dry mustard
½ tsp. paprika
Dash of cayenne

Put all the ingredients in a jar; cover and shake well to mix. Chill in the refrigerator. Shake it up again before using, as it may separate. Keeps best when stored in the refrigerator.

TABBOULI SALAD

"For we are the sweet fragrance of Christ [which exhales] unto God . . ." (2 Cor. 2:15 TAB).

Yield: 6 servings

1 cup cracked wheat bulgur
2 cups boiling water
2 lg. tomatoes, finely diced
1 bunch green onions and tops, finely chopped
3 Tbsp. chopped fresh mint leaves OR
2 Tbsp. dry mint leaves, crumbled
1 cup parsley, finely chopped
½ cup oil
1 tsp. honey
½ cup lemon juice
2 tsp. salt
Freshly ground pepper to taste
Romaine lettuce leaves

Place the cracked wheat bulgur in a bowl and cover with the boiling water. Allow to soak for about 1 hour. Drain off any excess water using a fine strainer. Return the bulgur to bowl and stir in the tomatoes, mint, onions and parsley. In a separate little bowl blend the oil, honey, lemon juice, salt and freshly ground pepper. (You might like to use your blender.) Add to the salad, mixing well. Chill in the refrigerator for at least 2 hours. Serve on individual salad plates lined with romaine leaves.

SAUERKRAUT SALAD

"A soft answer turneth away wrath: but grievous words stir up anger" (Prov. 16:1).

Yield: 8 to 10 servings

1 qt. sauerkraut, drained
1 cup celery, chopped
1 lg. green pepper, cut in small strips
1 cup green onions, chopped
1 cup honey
½ cup oil
½ cup apple cider vinegar

Place the thoroughly drained sauerkraut in a large bowl. Add the chopped celery, green pepper and green onions; stir until combined. Mix together the honey, oil, and vinegar either in your blender or else with electric beaters in a small mixing bowl. Add to the sauerkraut and vegetables. Cover and place in the refrigerator for at least 1 hour before serving. Any leftovers will keep nicely in the refrigerator for a day or two.

FIVE BEAN SALAD

"*. . . And as thy days, so shall thy strength be*" (Deut. 33:25).

Yield: 10 or 12 servings

1 (303) can cut green beans, drained
1 (303) can cut wax beans, drained
1 (303) can garbanzo beans, drained
1 (303) can kidney beans, drained
1 (303) can lima beans, drained
1 lg. sweet onion, sliced in rings
1 green pepper, sliced in rings
½ cup apple cider vinegar
½ cup vegetable oil
½ cup honey
2 tsp. salt
½ tsp. freshly ground pepper

Toss all the beans together with the onion rings and green pepper rings in a large bowl. In a separate little bowl beat together the apple cider vinegar, vegetable oil, honey, salt and freshly ground pepper. Stir in with the bean mixture. Allow to marinate at least 12 hours in the refrigerator. Store in glass only for top flavor. Five bean salad will keep for several days when refrigerated.

SPINACH-CASHEW SALAD

"I sought the Lord, and He heard me, and delivered me from all my fears" (Ps. 34:4).

Yield: 4 servings

1 bunch fresh spinach, washed and torn
2 oz. fresh mushrooms, cleaned and sliced
½ cup raw cashews, broken pieces
1 onion, sliced
¼ cup oil
1 tsp. honey
1 tsp. salt
1 Tbsp. apple cider vinegar
1 Tbsp. sesame seeds

Carefully wash the spinach leaves and stems. Drain off the excess water on a paper towel. Tear into bite-sized pieces, placing in a large bowl. Now use the damp paper towel to clean the mushrooms. Trim any brown spots off with a sharp knife. Do not use water on your fresh mushrooms. Add to the spinach. Now add the cashews and toss lightly. Set aside.

Combine the oil and honey in a frying pan. Saute the sliced onions in the oil mixture over medium low heat until they are just tender but not browned. Remove from the heat and stir in the salt and vinegar. Toss, mixing the oil evenly over the spinach. Sprinkle sesame seeds over the top. Serve in individual salad bowls or as desired. Delicious!! Spinach-Cashew Salad can be a meal in itself.

FRESH SPINACH SALAD

"If you are filled with light within, with no dark corners, then your face will be radiant too, as though a floodlight is beamed upon you" (Luke 11:36 TLB.)

Yield: 8 to 10 servings

2 bunches of fresh spinach
½ lb. fresh mung bean sprouts OR
1 can bean sprouts, drained
8 slices bacon, fried and crumbled
3 hard boiled eggs, chopped

Toss all the ingredients together in a large salad bowl. Serve immediately with HONEY-OF-A-DRESSING.

HONEY-OF-A-DRESSING

1 cup vegetable oil
¾ cup honey
⅓ cup catsup
¼ cup apple cider vinegar
1 Tbsp. Worcestershire sauce
1 med. sweet white onion, chopped

Mix the oil, honey, catsup, vinegar and Worcestershire sauce together in your blender until smooth. Empty the dressing into a small serving dish, then stir in the chopped sweet onion by hand. Let each person help themselves to as much HONEY-OF-A-DRESSING as desired. Store any leftover dressing in a tightly closed jar in the refrigerator.

ORANGE-HONEY FRENCH DRESSING

¼ cup frozen orange juice concentrate
¼ cup honey
1 Tbsp. vinegar
½ tsp. dry mustard
½ tsp. salt
⅔ cup salad oil

   Mix all ingredients except salad oil. Add the oil very slowly while beating constantly with a rotary or electric beater. Refrigerate until used. Calories per tablespoon: about 80. Delicious on all fruit salads.

I was rich in flowers and trees,
Humming-birds and honey-bees.

John Greenleaf Whittier (1807-1892)

RUSSIAN SALAD DRESSING

"Peace I leave with you, my peace I give unto you: not as the world giveth, give I unto you. Let not your heart be troubled, neither let it be afraid" (John 14:27).

¼ cup honey
½ cup apple cider vinegar
½ cup vegetable oil
½ cup catsup
2 Tbsp. onion, finely chopped

   Mix all the ingredients except the onions together in your blender or else in a small mixing bowl with your electric mixer. Process until well blended. Stir in the finely chopped sweet onion. Serve with tossed green salad. Store in a jar with a tight fitting lid in your refrigerator.

HONEY-CITRUS GELATIN

"For I know the plans I have for you, says the Lord. They are plans for good and not for evil, to give you a future and a hope" (Jer. 29:11 TLB).

Yield: 4 servings

½ cup cold water
1 envelope Knox gelatin
⅓ cup honey
1 cup citrus juice, made from juicing 1 lemon,
    1 lime and enough orange juice to fill up the cup
1 orange, sliced and quartered

Pour ½ cup of cold water into a small saucepan. Sprinkle the gelatin over the water. Then place over low heat, stirring constantly for about 3 minutes until the gelatin is completely dissolved. Add the honey and continue stirring until thoroughly blended. Remove the pan from the stove and stir in the citrus juice. Pour into 4 individual dessert goblets. Arrange the quartered orange slices artistically on top of each. Place in the refrigerator to chill until firm.

Variations: You can make all flavors of gelatin for either desserts or salads using real fruit juices, honey as the sweetener, and Knox gelatin. For every envelope of gelatin, use 1¾ cup of liquid, including the honey. Usually ¼ cup of honey is about right for most fruit juices. You can use more or less, depending on your personal taste and the sweetness of the juice.

HARVESTIME SALAD

". . . Behold, I say unto you, Lift up your eyes, and look on the fields; for they are white already to harvest" (John 4:35).

Yield: 4 servings

1 orange, peeled, sliced and quartered
2 stalks celery, sliced with leaves
1 big red apple, coarsely diced
1 cup red grapes, halved with seeds removed
¼ cup raisins
½ cup walnuts, broken pieces

Toss together and serve with the accompanying HONEY-CREAM DRESSING.

HONEY-CREAM DRESSING

½ cup mayonnaise
1 Tbsp. honey
1 Tbsp. apple cider vinegar
1 Tbsp. heavy cream
dash of salt

Stir together in the order listed. Keep in the refrigerator until ready to serve.

SUMMER SALAD

"Blessed be His glorious name for ever: and let the whole earth be filled with His glory: Amen and Amen" (Ps. 72:19).

Yield: about 4 servings

1 fresh peach, peeled and sliced
1 cup fresh blueberries
4 apricots, halved or quartered
1 cup watermelon balls
1 cup honeydew melon balls
1 cup Thompson seedless grapes

Chill all the fruit in advance. If possible, prepare just before serving. But if you're fixing summer salad for a picnic, you can prepare each fruit ahead of time and keep them from browning with a little sprinkle of "Fruit Fresh." Then wrap each type of fruit separately in plastic wrap. When you get to the picnic just put them all togther in a big bowl and gently stir to distribute evenly. Serve with a dressing made with equal amounts of honey and fresh lemon juice. Or for a richer alternative serve with the following APRICOT-HONEY DRESSING.

APRICOT-HONEY DRESSING

1 lb. can apricots, drained
¼ fresh lemon, seeded and peeled
1 thin strip of lemon rind (about 1" by 2")

¼ cup honey
Dash of salt
1 cup dairy sour cream

Put the drained apricots, lemon and rind into your blender. Put on the lid and process until the apricots are smooth. Add the honey, salt and sour cream. Cover and process only until well mixed. Serve with any fruit salad. Keep any leftover dressing in the refrigerator. This recipe makes about 2 cups of dressing.

MOLDED BLUEBERRY SALAD

"Acquaint now thyself with Him, and be at peace: thereby good shall come unto thee" (Job 22:21).

Yield: 8 servings

2 envelopes Knox gelatin
1 cup cold water
⅔ cup mild honey
1 lime, juiced
1 or 2 lemons, juiced
(⅔ cup fresh lemon-lime juice)
1⅓ cup cold water
1⅓ cup mayonnaise
1½ cup finely grated cabbage
1 cup blueberries
½ cup walnuts, finely chopped

Sprinkle the gelatin over 1 cup of cold water in a small saucepan. Place over low heat, stirring constantly until gelatin dissolves, for about 3 minutes. Remove from heat. Add the honey, ⅔ cup of freshly squeezed lemon-lime juice and the remaining 1⅓ cup of cold water. Chill in the refrigerator until lightly set. Whip in the mayonnaise. Then stir in the finely grated cabbage, the blueberries and the walnuts. Place in your favorite mold and chill in the refrigerator until firmly set.

OLD-FASHIONED RHUBARB SAUCE

"The just man walketh in his integrity; his children are blessed after him" (Prov. 20:7).

Yield: about 8 servings

4 cups finely diced rhubarb
1 cup honey

Wash the rhubarb stalks and split any large stalks in half lengthwise. Slice thinly into a large bowl. Add the honey and let stand for several hours or overnight. Do NOT add any water at all! The honey will draw the natural juices out of the rhubarb. Use more or less honey according to your personal taste. For a tarter sauce use only ¾ of a cup of honey. For a sweeter sauce you may use 1½ cups of honey, if desired. (We think one cup is just right.)

The next morning put the rhubarb and all its "juice" in a saucepan and bring to a boil. Then turn the heat down and simmer gently until the rhubarb is tender, 5 to 10 minutes. Do not overcook. Remove the sauce from the stove. Cover tightly and cool. It will be ready to eat within half an hour.

NOTE: If you are buying rhubarb remember that for every pound of fruit you will get 3¾ cups of finely diced rhubarb.

RAW CRANBERRY RELISH

"A man that hath friends must shew himself friendly: and there is a friend that sticketh closer than a brother" (Prov. 18:24).

Yield: 4 or 5 servings

1 orange
1 apple
2 cups raw cranberries
½ cup honey

Scrub the orange thoroughly. Cut in fourths with the peeling on. Process in your blender until all the peeling is well blended in. Or if you prefer, you can grind the orange in a food grinder. In that case, you would want to grate the orange peel first. Place the cranberries in the blender, about ½ cup at a time and chop finely. Here again you may use a food grinder if that's what you're equipped with. Place the finely chopped cranberries in a bowl with the orange pulp. Grate the apple with your carrot grater and stir in with the orange-cranberry mixture. Drizzle ½ cup of mild honey over the relish and stir until thoroughly mixed. Refrigerate for at least thirty minutes before serving. Better yet, make it up a day ahead of time. Raw cranberry relish is a colorful and tasty accompaniment to a turkey or ham dinner. It's one of our holiday favorites.

Meats & Vegetables

Serve immediately over steaming hot rice. The vegetables should still be a little crisp. Do not over cook.

SWEET 'N SOUR PORK

"And whatsoever ye do, do it heartily, as to the Lord, and not unto men" (Col. 3:23).

Yield: 4 to 6 servings

2 pork steaks, deboned and cut in small pieces
2 carrots, sliced
2 sticks celery, cut in large pieces
1 20-oz. can pineapple chunks, drained
1 green pepper, cut in long strips
¼ lb. fresh mushrooms (optional)
1 8-oz. can water chestnuts, drained and halved
1 lg. sweet onion, sliced

First of all, make the Sweet 'n Sour Sauce using the recipe below. Set aside, allowing to simmer. In a large skillet saute the pork which has been sliced very thinly. Cook until well-done. Prepare the carrots, celery, green pepper, onion and fresh mushrooms, if desired. Mix all the vegetables along with the drained pineapple chunks and water chestnuts in a large bowl. Add to the meat in the large skillet, stirring lightly to mix. Cover and cook over medium low heat for 3 to 5 minutes.

SWEET 'N SOUR SAUCE

4 cups water
1 cup soy sauce
⅓ cup vinegar
Juice from 20-oz. can of pineapple
1 cup brown sugar
1½ cups honey
1 can cream of chicken soup
½ cup tomato sauce
8 Tbsp. cornstarch
½ cup water

In a large heavy saucepan combine the water, soy sauce, vinegar, pineapple juice, brown sugar, honey, chicken soup and tomato sauce. Mix well with an electric mixer or by hand. Stir the cornstarch into half cup of water in a separate little bowl. Add to the sauce, blending thoroughly. Cook over medium low heat, stirring constantly until the sauce thickens. Allow to simmer until ready to serve. This sauce recipe is for a double batch. Freeze half of it. Then next time simply warm up the sauce.

MINTED LAMB CHOPS

"He brought me to the banqueting house, and his banner over me was love" (S. of S. 2:4).

Oven: broil   Yield: 4 servings

4 thick lamb chops
¼ cup lukewarm water
1 Tbsp. apple cider vinegar
Salt and pepper to taste
½ cup honey
2 Tbsp. chopped fresh mint leaves
  or 1 Tbsp. dried mint leaves

Combine the lukewarm water, vinegar, honey and chopped mint leaves in a saucepan. Simmer for five minutes. Season the lamb chops with salt and pepper to taste and place in a shallow baking pan. Broil in a preheated oven for five minutes, with the meat about four inches below the broiler. Spoon half of the mint sauce on top of the chops and return to the heat for another five minutes. Turn the chops and spoon on the remaining honey sauce. Lower the oven rack one position and return the chops to broil for another six to eight minutes, or until of desired doneness. Baste occasionally with the pan juice. Serve immediately.

JANE'S BEEF TERIYAKI

"Delight thyself also in the Lord; and He shall give thee the desires of thine heart" (Ps. 37:4).

Oven: 350°   Yield: 4 servings

1½ lbs. beef steak (flank or round)
¾ cup vegetable oil
¼ cup soy sauce
¼ cup honey
2 Tbsp. vinegar
2 Tbsp. finely chopped green onion
1 lg. clove garlic, minced
1½ tsp. ground ginger

Beat together the vegetable oil with the soy sauce, honey, vinegar and ginger till well-blended. Stir in the chopped green onions and the finely minced garlic. This is your marinate sauce. Place the steak in a glass baking dish and cover with the sauce. Marinate for 4 hours or longer — preferably overnight; turn occasionally. Now it is fully flavored and ready to cook — either on your barbeque or in the oven. When cooking it in the oven, cover with aluminum foil and bake for 45 minutes. Carve in thin slices, cutting on the diagonal. Serve with rice.

FESTIVE MEXICAN TAMALE PIE

" . . . In Your presence is fullness of joy, at Your right hand there are pleasures for evermore" (Ps. 16:11 TAB).

Oven: 375°   Yield: 6 servings

1 cup onion, chopped
1 sm. green pepper, chopped
1 Tbsp. vegetable oil
¾ lb. ground beef (lean)
2 8-oz. cans tomato sauce
1 12-oz. can whole kernel corn, drained
½ to 1 cup olives, chopped
1 clove garlic
1 Tbsp. honey
1 tsp. salt
2 tsp. chili powder
Dash of pepper
1½ cups cheddar cheese, shredded

Place the chopped onions and pepper in a skillet with the vegetable oil and cook till tender. Add the meat and brown, stirring occasionally. Now add the tomato sauce, corn, olives, garlic, honey, and seasonings. Simmer for 20 to 25 minutes, or until thick. Stir in the shredded cheese until it has melted. Pour into a buttered baking dish and top with corn meal topping.

CORN MEAL TOPPING
¾ cup yellow corn meal
½ tsp. salt
2 cups cold water
1 Tbsp. butter

Stir corn meal and salt into the cold water in a small sauce pan. Cook and stir until thick; add the butter. Spoon over meat mixture. Bake for 40 minutes. Serve with festive joy and a big tossed green salad.

CHICKEN TERIYAKI

"I love the Lord, Because He has heard (and now hears) my voice and my supplications" (Ps. 116:1 TAB).

Oven: 350°   Yield: 4 or 5 servings

4 lbs. frying chicken, cut up

¾ cup soy sauce

½ cup honey

1 clove garlic, minced

2 Tbsp. grated fresh ginger root

2 Tbsp. apple cider vinegar

Wash each piece of chicken carefully and pull away any excess fat to discard. Dry the pieces of chicken with a paper towel. Place the soy sauce, honey, minced garlic, grated ginger root, and apple cider vinegar in your blender and process till smooth. Arrange all the pieces of chicken in a large glass baking dish. Now pour the sauce from the blender over the chicken. Cover with plastic wrap and place in the refrigerator to marinate for at least 3 or 4 hours. Overnight is even better. Bake for one hour, turning the pieces of chicken over once when half way through the cooking time. Serve with rice and your favorite vegetable.

LASAGNE

" . . . she bringeth her food from afar" (Prov. 31:14).

Oven: 375°   Yield: 8 servings

1 lb. lean ground beef
1 sm. onion, chopped
1 sm. green pepper, chopped
2 cloves garlic, pressed
1 tsp. oregano
2 bay leaves
1 tsp. salt
1 tsp. honey
1 10½-oz. can tomato puree
1 15-oz. can tomato sauce
6 lasagne noodles
2 lbs. Ricotta cheese
¾ lb. Mozzarella cheese
Parmesan cheese

Brown the meat, onion and green pepper in a large skillet, breaking up the meat in small pieces. Add the garlic, seasonings, honey, tomato puree and tomato sauce. Rinse the cans with a little water and add to the mixture. Allow to simmer while cooking the noodles. Cook the lasagne noodles in a large pan of boiling water for 15 minutes, or until tender. Pour one-fourth the sauce into a 13"x9" pan. Place three of the noodles over the sauce. Next add half of the Ricotta cheese, then half of the Mozzarella cheese. Sprinkle with a generous amount of Parmesan cheese. Repeat layers, using half of the remaining sauce, and all the noodles and cheese. Pour remaining sauce over the top; sprinkle with Parmesan cheese. Bake for 25 minutes. Cut in squares and serve generous portions.

HONEYED PARSNIPS

"And one standing alone can be attacked and defeated, but two can stand back-to-back and conquer; three is even better, for a triple-braided cord is not easily broken" (Eccles. 4:12 TLB).

Oven: 350°   Yield: 5 or 6 servings

4 or 5 parsnips
½ cup honey
½ cup hot water
1 Tbsp. butter
Salt to taste

Wash and peel the parsnips. Boil in water salted to your taste until tender — about 10 minutes. Cut in half-inch diagonal slices and place in a baking dish. Whip the honey, hot water and butter together in a small bowl; then drizzle over the top of the parsnips. Bake for 10 minutes. Turn the parsnips over with a fork and bake for 10 additional minutes. If desired, just before serving, brown additionally under the broiler. But watch very closely all the time to prevent from scorching!

BAKED LENTILS WITH HONEY

"Your words are a flashlight to light the path ahead of me, and keep me from stumbling" (Ps. 119:105 TLB).

Oven: 325°   Yield: 6 servings

2 cups lentils
6 bacon slices, cut in small pieces
1 lb. pork sausage
½ cup chopped onion
¼ cup finely chopped chutney
1 tsp. salt
1 tsp. mustard
½ cup honey

Cook the lentils in a large pan with 4 cups of cold water. When they come to a boil, lower the heat to simmer and cook with a lid on for one hour. Drain off any liquid that is left. Meanwhile, fry the sausage, disregarding the grease. Preheat the oven. Into the lentils stir together the bacon, chutney, onion, salt, mustard, sausage and one cup of water. Empty out into a 2-quart shallow baking dish. Drizzle the honey all over the top. Cover and bake for 45 minutes. Remove cover and bake 30 minutes more. Lentils are rich in protein. A delightful change from traditional baked beans.

HONEY BAKED BEANS

"This is the day which the Lord hath made; we will rejoice and be glad in it" (Ps. 118:24).

Oven: 300°   Yield: 6 to 8 servings

2 cups dried beans (kidney or navy)
6 to 8 slices bacon
1 tsp. ginger
1 sm. sweet onion, chopped
½ cup honey
½ cup catsup
1 tsp. salt
1 tsp. dry mustard

Wash the dry beans, then place them to soak in a quart of warm water for three hours. Simmer over low heat in a tightly covered saucepan for one hour and fifteen minutes. Do not actually let them come to a boil, but simmer just below the boiling point. Drain the beans, saving the water. Place the bacon, which you have cut in one-inch pieces in the bottom of your bean pot (or large baking dish) and pour the drained beans on top. In a separate bowl combine the bean water with the ginger, chopped onion, honey, catsup, salt and dry mustard. Pour over the top of the beans. Place the rest of the bacon pieces on top. Cover with a lid or aluminum foil and let bake for 5 or 6 hours. Stir occasionally, and if the beans become too dry, add a little boiling water.

GARBANZO-MEATBALL STEW

"But thanks be to God, Who in Christ always leads us in triumph — as trophies of Christ's victory — and through us spreads and makes evident the fragrance of the knowledge of God everywhere" (2 Cor. 2:14 TAB).

Yield: 4 to 5 servings

1½ lbs. lean ground beef
2 Tbsp. oil
1 15-oz. can tomato sauce
2 Tbsp. honey
2 cloves garlic, minced
1 cup chopped onion
2 - 15-oz. cans Garbanzo
    beans, drained (3½ cups)
3 cups diced fresh zucchini
1 cup diced fresh tomato
1 tsp. salt
Fresh ground pepper to taste

Shape the ground beef into one-inch balls and brown in a large skillet with the oil. Turn to brown on all sides. Remove meatballs from skillet and set aside. In the same skillet stir together the tomato sauce, honey, garlic, onions, salt and freshly ground pepper. Add the Garbanzo beans, which you have drained. Cover and allow to simmer for 30 to 60 minutes. This is a great meal to fix when you're uncertain of the exact dinner hour; or this much can be prepared ahead of time. Return the meatballs to the skillet mixture. Bring to simmer, adding just a little water if needed. Add the zucchini and fresh tomatoes, stirring in gently, then simmer for about 10 minutes. Do not overcook the zucchini — it should be just slightly crisp. Serve immediately while piping hot. Garbanzo-Meatball Stew is a meal in itself. Serve generous portions with a loaf of fresh homemade bread.

MINTED CARROTS

"Hope in God: for I shall yet praise Him, Who is the health of my countenance, and my God" (Ps. 43:5).

Yield: 4 or 5 servings

5 or 6 medium-sized carrots
¼ cup butter
2 tsp. chopped fresh mint leaves
3 Tbsp. honey

Scrub the carrots clean with a vegetable brush. Cut in strips. Steam until tender; then drain. While the carrots are steaming, combine the butter, honey and mint leaves together in a small saucepan, stirring until the butter has melted. Add the honey mint sauce to the hot, well-drained carrots; heat over low temperature and stir occasionally till the carrots are glazed. Minted carrots are a nice side dish to serve along beside lamb or beef.

SPARERIBS WITH BARBECUE SAUCE

"O bless our God, ye people, and make the voice of his praise to be heard" (Ps. 66:8).

Oven: 350°   Yield: 4 servings

3 lbs. spareribs (country-style, if available)
Salt and pepper
Paprika
1 Tbsp. vegetable oil
1 lg. onion, sliced
¼ cup catsup
2 Tbsp. apple cider vinegar
1 tsp. Worcestershire sauce
⅛ tsp. chili powder
¼ tsp. celery seed
½ cup water
1 Tbsp. honey

Cut the ribs into serving pieces. Season with salt, pepper and paprika. Brown the ribs in a skillet with the oil, turning to brown all sides. In the meantime, in another saucepan, stir together the catsup, vinegar, chili powder, celery seed, water and honey with the sliced onions. Then let the sauce simmer while the meat is browning. When the ribs are brown, place in a baking dish and pour the simmering hot sauce on top. Bake for 1 hour, basting frequently with the sauce. (If you

have a pressure cooker you can cook the same dish in 15 minutes.) Serve with steaming hot mountains of mashed potatoes.

KIDNEY BEANS SUPREME

"... Yes, happy — blessed, fortunate, prosperous (to be envied) — is the people whose God is the Lord! (Ps. 144:15 TAB).

Yield: 8 to 10 servings

3 cups dry kidney beans
1 med. onion, minced
1 green pepper, minced
1 clove garlic, crushed & minced
1 lb. ground beef, browned
¼ cup catsup
¼ cup honey
2 tsp. salt
1 cup bean liquid
1 qt. stewed tomatoes, with juice
Freshly ground pepper to taste

Soak the kidney beans in 5 cups of water for 24 hours, or at least overnight. The next day drain off the water and reserve the "bean liquid." In a large, heavy saucepan combine the beans with the finely minced onion, green pepper and garlic. Add the ground beef which you have browned till well done in a skillet. Stir the catsup and honey together in a separate little bowl; add to the beans. Add the salt and the liquid you reserved from off the beans along with one quart of stewed tomatoes. Grind in a little fresh pepper according to your taste. Simmer slowly for two or three hours, stirring occasionally. This is a great dish to fix on a chilly day. We like to let it simmer all afternoon on our little wood stove.

BAKED ACORN SQUASH

"The eternal God is thy refuge, and underneath are the everlasting arms" (Deut. 33:27).

Oven: 350°   Yield: 2 servings

1 Acorn squash
2 Tbsp. honey
¼ tsp. salt
Freshly ground pepper to taste
2 tsp. butter
6 sausage links, browned

Wash the squash and cut in half lengthwise. Remove the seeds. Bake cut side down in a shallow pan for 35 to 40 minutes, or until almost tender. In the meantime, fry the link sausage over medium low heat, turning frequently until browned. Drain off excess fat on paper towels. Turn the hot acorn squash cut side up and sprinkle with salt. Brush each half with a teaspoon of butter, then drizzle each with a tablespoon of honey. Last of all, place three little browned sausage links in each hole. Return to the oven and bake for 25 more minutes.

HOLIDAY HAM WITH HONEY-ORANGE GLAZE

"For unto us a child is born, unto us a Son is given: and the government shall be upon His shoulder: and His name shall be called Wonderful, Counselor, the mighty God, The everlasting Father, The Prince of Peace" (Isa. 9:6).

Oven: 325°

10 to 12 lb. ham, fully cooked
1 6 oz. can frozen orange juice, thawed
¼ cup prepared mustard
¼ cup honey
½ cup butter or margarine
1 clove garlic, crushed
1 Tbsp. soy sauce
2 Tbsp. apple juice
½ tsp. ground ginger

Buy a fully cooked ham that is ready to be heated for serving. Bake for a total of three hours. Before the last 30 minutes of the baking time, remove the ham from the oven and score the ham fat in diamond shape designs, cutting only ¼-inch deep. Stud with whole cloves, if desired. Then baste with the HONEY-ORANGE SAUCE, spooning the glaze over 2 or 3 times. Return to oven 30 minutes.

To make the sauce, heat in a small saucepan the orange juice concentrate, mustard, honey, butter and garlic. Stir and cook over low heat until the butter has melted. Stir in the soy sauce, apple juice and ginger. Cook over low heat till thoroughly heated. Actually, this sauce is universal in appeal. You can use it on baked chicken, game hens or spare-ribs as well.

HARVARD BEETS

"Ask, and it shall be given you; seek, and ye shall find; knock, and it shall be opened unto you" (Matt. 7:7).

Yield: 5 servings

2 cups diced beets
2 Tbsp. honey
1 Tbsp. cornstarch
¼ tsp. salt
¼ cup apple cider vinegar
2 Tbsp. butter or margarine

Scrub and dice about one pound of beets or enough to make two cups when diced. Cook in a small amount of water until tender. Drain beets, saving ⅓ cup of the liquid. In a saucepan combine the honey, cornstarch and salt. Stir in the reserved beet juice, the vinegar and butter. Cook and stir until the mixture becomes thick. Add the cooked beets to the hot honey sauce and simmer over low heat until piping hot. Harvard beets are a delicious side dish to serve with roast beef and mashed potatoes.

BORSCH

"It is better to eat soup with someone you love than steak with someone you hate" (Prov. 15:17 TLB).

Serves: 4

4 sm. beets, diced
1 sm. onion, thinly sliced
3 cups water
2 cups stewed tomatoes
2 cups finely sliced cabbage
1 tsp. salt
1 cup diced roast beef or left-over steak
2 Tbsp. honey
2 Tbsp. apple cider vinegar

Scrub the beets clean and dice in small pieces. Put in a large saucepan with the onion slices and the water. Cover and bring to a boil. Then turn to simmer and cook for 10 minutes till beets are tender. Now add the tomatoes, cabbage, salt, diced beef, honey and vinegar. Stir well. Simmer for another 15 minutes. Top with a little freshly ground pepper. Place in soup bowls and if desired top off each bowl with a little sour cream.

"Borsch" is a tasty Russian soup colored red with beet juice. There are probably as many versions as there are apple pies. This one is special enough to serve your best friend for lunch. And it's a sure winner when accompanied with a loaf of freshly baked bread.

AUTUMN APPLE PORK CHOPS

". . . Put in your sickle and reap, because the hour to reap has come, because the harvest of the earth is ripe" (Rev. 14:15).

Oven: 350°

6 lean loin pork chops
Salt
1½ tsp. sage, divided
3 tart apples
3 Tbsp. molasses
3 Tbsp. honey
3 Tbsp. all-purpose flour
2 cups hot water
1 Tbsp. vinegar
⅓ cup seedless raisins (optional)

Rub the pork chops with a mixture of ¼ teaspoon salt and ¼ teaspoon sage and slowly brown in a teflon pan. (You may use a pan sprayed with PAM if you wish.) When crisp place the chops in a shallow baking dish. Do not wash the pan.

Peel, core, and slice apples about ¼-inch thick and arrange over the pork chops. Drizzle the molasses and honey over the apples.

Go back to the pan you browned the chops in and if necessary add a touch of butter and sprinkle with flour; cook until brown, stirring occasionally. Slowly add the hot water, stirring constantly until smooth; bring to a rolling boil and add: vinegar, ½ teaspoon salt and the raisins. Pour this mixture over the chops and apples. Cover and bake for 1 hour. Serves 6.

I often prepare my favorite bread dressing and line the baking dish with it before I add the chops. This gives a more complete touch to the meal.

MACARONI AND CHEESE

" 'I will lead My flock and I will lead them to rest,' declares the Lord God" (Ezek. 34:15).

Oven: 375°

½ lb. cooked macaroni
3 eggs, separated
¼ cup margarine
2 Tbsp. honey
2 cups cottage cheese
1 cup yogurt or sour cream
½ cup wheat germ or bread crumbs

Beat the three egg yolks and mix with margarine, honey, cottage cheese and yogurt. Beat egg whites until stiff. Fold all the ingredients together until evenly mixed, except the wheat germ. Pour into an oiled 2-quart casserole. Top with wheat germ or bread crumbs, dot with butter. Bake for 45 minutes. A delicious variation of an old favorite.

CURRIED CABBAGE AND MEATBALLS

"Both riches and honor come from Thee, and Thou dost rule over all, and in Thy hand is power and might; and it lies in Thy hand to make great, and to strengthen everyone. Now therefore, our God, we thank Thee, and praise Thy glorious name" (1 Chron. 29:12-13).

CABBAGE
1 med. head of cabbage
1 can of tomatoes (15½ ozs.)
1 med. onion, finely chopped
1 diced apple (opt.)
½ cup raisins (opt.)

MEATBALLS
1 lb. hamburger
1 med. egg
½ cup raw rice
½ tsp. salt

SAUCE
1 8 oz. can of tomato sauce
½ cup water
⅓ cup lemon juice
½ cup honey
½ tsp. salt
1½ tsp. curry powder

Shred the cabbage coarsely and dice the tomatoes. Then simmer cabbage, tomatoes with their liquid, and onion in a heavy skillet (an electric skillet is super) for 15 minutes, occasionally spooning liquid over the cabbage to wilt it.

While cabbage is cooking, mix the meat ingredients. Form them into 1 inch balls.

Combine all the sauce ingredients and mix well. When the cabbage is wilted, pour the sauce over it. Add meatballs, making sure that they are covered with liquid. Simmer constantly until the rice in the meatballs is tender (approximately 45 minutes - 1 hour).

CHICKEN WITH A DIFFERENCE

"I will give thanks to the Lord with all my heart; I will tell of all Thy wonders, I will be glad and exult in Thee; I will sing praise to Thy name, O most High" (Ps. 9:1-2).

Oven: 350°

1 2½-3 lb. fryer, cut up
⅓ cup melted margarine or butter
⅓ cup honey
1 tsp. curry powder
1 tsp. salt
2 Tbsp. prepared mustard (Dijon preferably)

Place the chicken in a baking pan, skin-side up in a single layer. Combine the rest of the ingredients and pour over chicken. Baste chicken every 10-15 minutes. Bake until chicken is well browned and tender (approximately 1¼ hours).

Cakes

CARROT CAKE

"My son, honey whets the appetite, and so does wisdom! When you enjoy becoming wise, there is hope for you! A bright future lies ahead!" (Prov. 24:13, 14 TLB).

Oven: 325°

1 cup vegetable oil
1 cup honey
4 eggs
1 cup whole wheat flour
1 cup white flour
2 tsp. cinnamon
2 tsp. baking soda
½ tsp. salt
½ cup coconut
¾ cup walnuts, chopped
3 cups carrots, grated

In a large mixing bowl beat together the oil, honey and eggs until the mixture is light and fluffy. In another smaller bowl combine the flours with the other dry ingredients and then stir in the coconut and chopped walnuts. Stir all the dry ingredients into the honey mixture by hand until well blended, then mix with your electric mixer for about 2 minutes. Stir in the grated carrots by hand until thoroughly mixed. Pour into a greased and floured 9"x13" loaf pan or, if you desire, three 1-pound empty tin cans. Bake for 60 minutes. Cool in the pans for 10 minutes before turning out. Finish cooling on a rack. Wrap well and refrigerate at least one day before serving. It's fine without any frosting but if you want to dress it up good, here's a topping for the sweetest tooth:

COCONUT FROSTING

8 oz. cream cheese, softened
⅓ cup butter, softened at room temperature
2 tsp. vanilla
½ cup honey
½ cup finely grated coconut (unsweetened)
¼ cup chopped walnuts

Mix all the ingredients together in a small bowl in the order listed. Spread on cooled cake. Chill in the refrigerator before serving.

Sweet is the breath of vernal shower,
The bee's collected treasures sweet,
Sweet music's melting fall, but sweeter
   yet
The still small voice of gratitude.

Thomas Gray (1716-1771)

GINGERBREAD

"How great is Your goodness which You have laid up for those who fear, revere and worship You . . . (Ps. 31:19 TAB).

Oven: 325°

2 cups white flour
¾ cup whole wheat flour
1 tsp. soda
2 tsp. baking powder
1 tsp. salt
1 tsp. cinnamon
1 tsp. ground ginger
¾ cup honey
¾ cup molasses
1 cup vegetable oil
1 egg, unbeaten
1 cup buttermilk

Measure out the flours, baking soda, baking powder, salt and spices in a mixing bowl. Stir together until the mixture is thoroughly blended. In another bowl place the oil, honey, molasses, and egg and beat with an electric mixer till light and creamy. If you measure the oil first in the same cup as the honey it will come out "slick as a whistle." Now add the flour alternately with the buttermilk, beating after each addition until smooth. Bake in a well-greased 9" by 13" baking pan for 55 minutes or until done when tested with a tooth-pick. (The toothpick should come out clean). Serve with whipped cream, sweetened with honey and a tablespoon of grated orange rind.

ORANGE-HONEY CAKE

". . . and, lo, I am with you alway, even unto the end of the world" (Matt. 28:20).

Oven: 325°

1½ cubes butter or margarine, melted and cooled
1⅓ cups honey
2 eggs
½ cup milk
2 Tbsp. lemon juice
3½ cups white flour
1 tsp. ground cloves
¼ tsp. salt
¾ tsp. baking soda
⅔ cup diced candied orange peel
1 cup coarsely chopped walnuts

In a large bowl beat together the melted butter with the honey, eggs, milk, and lemon juice. Beat until well blended. Set aside. In another bowl, stir together the flour, cloves, salt, and baking soda. Stir the flour mixture into the honey mixture, then beat for 2 to 3 minutes until the mixture is light and creamy. Mix in the candied orange peel and nuts. Pour into a greased and floured 8½"x3" spring form cake pan, OR you may bake in two 8½"x4½" loaf pans. Spread the batter evenly with a spatula. Tap the bottom of the pan sharply against a hard surface several times to settle batter. Then bake. In the spring form pan the baking time is 1 hour and 20 minutes. In loaf pans, you'll bake for 1 hour and 10 minutes. The cake is done when a skewer inserted in the center comes out clean. Cool in the spring form pan 20 minutes before removing from the pan. The loaves should cool 10 minutes. Finish cooling on wire racks and frost with EASY ORANGE FROSTING if desired. This cake is rich and heavy, and resembles fruitcake. You'll enjoy it for the holidays. Keeps well in the refrigerator.

EASY ORANGE FROSTING
⅓ cup butter, softened to room temperature
½ cup mild honey
¼ cup frozen orange juice concentrate
1 cup non-instant dry milk powder

Beat together in a small mixing bowl till well blended. Spread over cooled cake. Sprinkle with chopped nuts, if desired.

HONEY-CAROB CAKE

"Charm and grace are deceptive, and beauty is vain (because it is not lasting), but a woman who reverently and worshipfully fears the Lord, she shall be praised!" (Prov. 31:30 TAB).

Oven: 350°

2 cups white flour, sifted
1½ tsp. baking soda
½ cup butter or margarine, softened to
    room temperature
1¼ cups honey
2 eggs
¾ cup carob powder, sifted
1 tsp. vanilla
⅔ cup water

Sift the flour and baking soda together in a small bowl. In another bowl, cream the softened butter, then add the honey gradually, pouring about a tablespoon-ful each time, beating well after each addition, to keep the batter thick. Add about one-fourth of the flour mixture; beat until smooth. Add the eggs, one at a time, beating well after each. Blend in the sifted carob powder and the vanilla. Add the rest of the flour, alter-nately with the water, beginning and ending with flour; beat about three minutes. Bake in a greased and floured 9"x13" pan for about 45 minutes or until done. Test with a toothpick in the center of the hot cake. When it's done, the toothpick will come out clean. Makes one large loaf. Let cool for ½ hour before frosting with QUICK HONEY PECAN ICING.

QUICK HONEY PECAN ICING
3 Tbsp. shortening
3 Tbsp. butter
⅓ cup honey
¾ cup chopped pecans

In a small saucepan combine the shortening, butter, and honey, and bring to a boil over medium-low heat. Remove from the heat and stir in the pecans. Place the hot pan in a sink of cold water and stir until the icing thickens. Spread on cake. Toast very lightly under a broiler, just until the icing bubbles. Watch carefully! Makes enough to frost a 9"x13" cake.

SOURDOUGH-CAROB CAKE

"God is our refuge and strength, a very present help in trouble. Therefore will not we fear..." (Ps. 46:1,2).

Oven: 325°

½ cup thick sourdough starter

1 cup warm water

¾ cup dry powdered milk

1½ cups flour

¾ cup honey

½ cup butter or margarine, softened

½ tsp. salt

⅔ cup carob powder or cocoa

1½ tsp. baking soda

1 tsp. vanilla

1 tsp. cinnamon

2 eggs

Mix together the sourdough starter with the warm water, powdered milk and flour in a mixing bowl. Cover, and allow to sit in a warm place for 2 to 3 hours, or until the mixture smells yeasty and is nice and bubbly. In a separate bowl, cream the honey together with the softened butter. Add the spices and the carob powder, stirring until well blended. Add the eggs, one at a time, beating after each addition. Now add this honey mixture to the sourdough mixture and mix for about 1 minute on low with an electric beater. Pour into 2 round layer pans lined with waxed paper. Bake for 35 to 40 minutes, being careful to make sure the cake is done before removing it from oven. Allow to cool for 10 minutes in the pans before turning out on cake racks to finish cooling. Frost with HONEY CREAM ICING, topped off with about ¼ cup of carob chips sprinkled on top.

HONEY CREAM ICING

8 oz. cream cheese, softened to room temperature

⅓ cup honey

1 tsp. vanilla

Stir the honey together with the softened cream cheese and vanilla until smooth. Spread on cake. Decorate with carob chips if desired.

CAROB-CHIP ZUCCHINI CAKE

"There is a right time for everything . . . A time to plant; A time to harvest" (Eccles. 3:1-2 TLB).

Oven: 325°

½ cup margarine, softened
¼ cup vegetable oil
1 cup honey

2 eggs
1 tsp. vanilla
½ cup sour milk
1 cup whole wheat flour
1½ cups white flour
¼ cup carob powder (or cocoa)
½ tsp. baking powder
1 tsp. baking soda
½ tsp. cinnamon
½ tsp. cloves
2 cups shredded zucchini
¼ cup carob chips (or chocolate chips)

In a large mixing bowl cream together the softened margarine with the oil, honey, eggs and vanilla, beating until light and fluffy. Add the sour milk and mix well. If you have no sour milk on hand, a teaspoonful of apple cider vinegar in a ½ cup of sweet milk will quickly do the trick. In a separate bowl stir together all the dry ingredients, mixing very thoroughly, making especially sure to break up any lumps of carob powder. Stir the dry ingredients into the honey mixture, then mix with your electric mixer for about 2 minutes. By hand, stir in the zucchini which you have shredded with your carrot grater. Empty out the batter into a greased and floured 9"x13" baking pan. Sprinkle the batter with carob chips. Bake for 40 to 45 minutes or until done. No need to frost this cake because the carob or chocolate chips melt to form an incredibly tempting topping.

CRANBERRY CHEESE CAKE

"Be strong and of a good courage; be not afraid, neither be thou dismayed: for the Lord thy God is with thee whithersoever thou goest" (Josh. 1:9).

Oven: 325°   Yield: 12 to 16 servings

2 8 oz. pkg. cream cheese, softened to
    room temperature
4 eggs
½ cup mild honey

⅛ tsp. almond extract
1 pt. sour cream mixed with 3 Tbsp. honey and
    1 Tbsp. vanilla

Cranberry Glaze:
1 can whole cranberry sauce
2 Tbsp. honey
1 Tbsp. cornstarch
1 Tbsp. grated lemon rind
1 Tbsp. lemon juice

Place the softened cream cheese in a mixing bowl and beat until smooth and creamy. Add the eggs, one at a time, beating well after each addition. Thoroughly blend in the almond extract and the ½ cup of honey. Pour into a lightly-buttered 9" pie pan and bake for 50 minutes. Set aside to cool for 20 minutes. Spread the sour cream mixture over the warm, baked cheese layer and return to the oven for another 15 minutes. Remove from the oven and thoroughly chill. Cover the chilled pie with cooled cranberry glaze made by heating together the cranberry sauce, honey, cornstarch, lemon rind, and lemon juice. Cook over low heat in a heavy saucepan, stirring constantly until thick and clear. Cool. Spread on top of cheese cake leaving about ½" sour cream showing on sides. Keep in the refrigerator until ready to serve. The flavor actually improves as the cheese cake ages in the refrigerator. But don't worry, it won't be around very long! CRANBERRY CHEESE CAKE is a perfect dessert for your most festive holiday meal.

BANANA SPICE CAKE

"My fruit is better than gold, even pure gold, and my yield than choicest silver" (Prov. 8:19).

Oven: 350°   Yield: 12 servings

1 cup honey
½ cup oil
3 eggs
2 tsp. vanilla
½ cup buttermilk
2 cups whole wheat flour (pastry)
½ cup white flour
½ cup instant dry milk powder
½ cup wheat germ
4 tsp. baking powder
1 tsp. salt
1 tsp. cinnamon
½ tsp. nutmeg
½ tsp. allspice
1½ cups mashed bananas (3 medium)
⅔ cup chopped nuts

Cream together the honey and the oil. Add the eggs, one at a time, beating well after each addition. Mix in the vanilla and buttermilk. In a separate bowl sift the flours, dry milk powder, wheat germ, baking powder, salt, and spices. Add the dry ingredients to the honey mix and beat well. Blend in the mashed bananas and the nuts. Bake in a greased and floured 9"x13" pan 45 minutes. Frost with the HONEY BUTTERCREAM ICING.

HONEY BUTTERCREAM ICING
2 Tbsp. soft butter
¼ cup honey
1 tsp. vanilla
3 Tbsp. buttermilk
1 cup instant powdered milk

Blend butter, honey and vanilla. Add powdered milk and buttermilk, alternately adjusting ingredients if necessary to reach a desired consistency. If desired, dust with a dash of cinnamon or nutmeg.

ADAM AND EVE'S HONEY-OF-A-FIG CAKE

"Now learn the parable from the fig tree: when its branch has already become tender, and puts forth its leaves, you know that summer is near; even so you too, when you see all these things, recognize that He is near, right at the door" (Matt. 24:32-33).

Oven: 300-325°

2 cups self-rising flour (if plain flour add ¾ tsp. salt)
1½ tsp. baking soda

3 whole eggs
1 cup honey
½ cup vegetable oil
½ cup buttermilk
1 Tbsp. butter flavoring
1 cup chopped pecans
1 cup chopped fig preserves

Put all of the ingredients together in a mixing bowl and mix until well blended. Pour into a greased and floured tube pan and bake approximately 1 hour and 10 minutes.

HONEY-OF-A-FIG CAKE GLAZE
½ stick butter (or margarine)
¼ cup honey
¼ cup buttermilk
½ Tbsp. molasses
½ Tbsp. vanilla
¼ tsp. butter flavoring

Mix all the ingredients together in a small saucepan and bring to a boil. Take the cake out of the oven and while it is still hot, pour the glaze over the top. Leave in the pan until cool. Serves 12. It's a tantalizing flavor which will send your sweet-tooth into rhapsody.

LEMON COTTAGE CHEESE CAKE

"All the days of the afflicted are bad, but a cheerful heart has a continual feast" (Prov. 15:15).

Oven: 350°   Yield: 8 servings

2 cups cottage cheese (16 oz.)
1 cup yogurt (lemon optional)
3 egg yolks
1 tsp. vanilla
1 Tbsp. lemon juice plus grated
   rind of one lemon
½ cup honey
¼ tsp. salt
¼ cup whole wheat flour
3 egg whites
9-inch graham cracker crust in spring form pan

Blend the cottage cheese, yogurt, egg yolks, vanilla and lemon juice and lemon rind. Mix in the honey. Mix flour and salt and add to the mix. Beat the egg whites until stiff and fold into the honey mix. Pour into the crust and bake until the center is firm. Loosen the cake sides but do not remove from the pan until the cake is cool. Serve with a topping of fresh berries and your family will stand up and cheer.

Pies

PECAN PIE

"...for the joy of the Lord is your strength" (Neh. 8:10).

Oven: 400°   Yield: about 8 pieces

1 (9-inch) unbaked pastry shell
3 eggs
1 cup honey
1 tsp. vanilla
1 Tbsp. butter, melted and cooled
¼ tsp. salt
1 cup broken pecans

Line a 9-inch pie pan with your favorite pastry. Chill in the refrigerator while proceeding to make the filling. Preheat oven. Beat the eggs with your electric beater until light and foamy. Add the honey, vanilla, butter and salt and continue beating until smooth. Stir in the nuts. Pour into the cooled pastry shell and bake for 10 minutes. Then turn the oven down to 300 degrees and bake for 20 more minutes. Last of all, turn the oven to 250 and continue baking for five minutes. Test to see if the pie is done by inserting a silver knife in the center of the filling — if it's done it will come out clean. If not, cook another 5 minutes. Cool before serving.

ONE CRUST RHUBARB PIE

"...and the little hills rejoice on every side" (Ps. 65:12).

Oven: 375°   Yield: 6 servings

¾ cup honey
1 Tbsp. soft butter
¼ cup flour
1 egg, slightly beaten
⅓ cup water
4 cups rhubarb, cut in ½" pieces
1 unbaked pastry shell

Stir the honey together with the butter and flour until smooth. Add the slightly beaten egg and the water and beat with the electric beaters until well-blended. Pour over the cut up rhubarb and let set in a bowl while you make the pie crust. When the crust is ready pour the rhubarb mixture into the shell. Bake for 45 minutes. Let cool until it has thickened. This one crusted rhubarb pie is especially delicious when served with honey-sweetened whipped cream. And for those of you who really never cared much for rhubarb because of its tartness, I guarantee you'll have a brand new surprise in store when you take your first bite of this version of rhubarb pie.

MILE HIGH BANANA PIE

"A wise woman builds her house, while a foolish woman tears hers down by her own efforts" (Prov. 14:1 TLB).

Yield: about 8 servings

3 bananas

3 egg whites, stiffly beaten

4 Tbsp. corn starch

¾ cup honey

2 cups boiling water

1 tsp. vanilla

½ pint whipping cream

9-inch pastry shell (baked)

Slice three bananas into a cooled 9-inch pastry shell. Beat three egg whites until very stiff; set aside. In a medium-sized saucepan stir together the cornstarch, honey and boiling water. Cook until the mixture thickens, stirring constantly. Remove from the heat and stir in the vanilla. Now pour the hot mixture over the stiffly beaten egg whites and beat at the highest speed with your electric mixer for about ten minutes, or until stiff. Pour over the bananas. Beat the whipping cream till thick and spread on top of the pie. If desired, you can garnish with slivered almonds. Chill for several hours before serving.

FRESH STRAWBERRY PIE

"Jesus said unto him, If thou canst believe, all things are possible to him that believeth" (Mark 9:23).

Yield: 6 to 8 servings

4 cups whole strawberries, washed and stemmed

1 8-inch baked pastry shell

Glaze:

½ cup mild flavored honey

⅓ cup water

1 Tbsp. Knox gelatin

3 drops red food coloring

Filling:

1 pkg. (8 oz.) cream cheese

1 tsp. milk

¼ tsp. salt

2 Tbsp. honey

2 Tbsp. freshly squeezed orange juice

Wash the strawberries gently in cold water (but do not allow them to soak!). Remove the stems. Crush one cup berries. In saucepan, mix together ½ cup honey, water, gelatin, crushed strawberries and food coloring. Cook over medium heat, stirring constantly, until clear and thickened (takes from 10 to 15 minutes). Set aside to cool until mixture mounds. In small bowl, cream together the cream cheese, milk, salt and 2 tablespoons honey. Spread over baked, chilled pastry shell. Chill. Gently toss remaining 3 cups of whole strawberries with the fresh orange juice. Let stand about 30 minutes. Arrange over filling in the pastry shell. Spoon cooled glaze over berries. Refrigerate until well chilled (for about 3 hours). Serve with honey-sweetened whipped cream.

WILD BLACKBERRY PIE

"The Lord liveth; and blessed be my rock; and let the God of my salvation be exalted" (Ps. 18:46).

Oven: 425°   Yield: about 8 pieces

4 cups fresh or frozen berries (unsweetened)

1 tsp. lemon juice

4 Tbsp. flour

⅔ cup honey

2 Tbsp. butter or margarine

Pastry for double 9-inch crust

Line a 9-inch pie pan with your favorite pastry and roll out the top crust. Put the wild blackberries in a large bowl and sprinkle with lemon juice. Add the flour and stir into the berries until the flour is coating all of the berries. Now spoon the berries into the unbaked pie shell, pour the honey all over the top and dot with butter. Cover with the top crust, pinching the edges together to seal. Make a few decorative slits for the steam to escape. Cover the edges of the crust with 2-inch strips of aluminum foil to prevent from over-browning. Bake in the center of the oven for about 45 minutes or until the crust is lightly browned. Delicious served warm. But don't cut the pie while it is hot or it will not hold it's shape — wait until it is just a little warm. This recipe is adaptable to any of the various types of berries that might be available in your area, such as: loganberries, boysenberries, huckleberries or blueberries. If you are using the red huckleberries omit the lemon juice because these berries are a little more tart in themselves. Happy berry picking!

STRAWBERRY CREAM FREEZER PIE

"Kind words are like honey — enjoyable and healthful" (Prov. 16:24 TLB).

1½ cups heavy cream
¼ cup honey
1 tsp. vanilla
1 cup plain yogurt
1½ cups sliced strawberries
  (fresh or frozen)

Whip the cream in a chilled bowl till thick. Add the honey slowly, beating all the time. Add the vanilla and beat till mixed in. Pour about one cup of the whipped cream in your blender. Add to this the sliced strawberries and blend till smooth. Stir in with the rest of the whipped cream mixture. Add the yogurt and beat with electric beater till thoroughly mixed. Pour into a big 9-inch pie shell. Our favorite is the COCONUT PIE SHELL. Cover with plastic wrap and place in the freezer for at least three hours before serving. If desired, top with a few freshly sliced strawberries when serving.

COCONUT PIE SHELL

1 cup finely shredded coconut (unsweetened)
½ cup wheat germ
1½ Tbsp. honey
1½ Tbsp. vegetable oil

Combine all the ingredients. Pat and press evenly into a 9" pie pan. Chill in the freezer about 15 minutes till firm. Fill with your favorite cream pie. This is a great recipe for those hot summer days when you'd rather not heat up the kitchen with your oven.

How doth the busy little bee
Improve each shining hour
And gather honey all the day
From every opening flower!

Isaac Watts (1674-1748)

LEMON CHIFFON PIE

"And I heard a great voice out of heaven saying, Behold, the tabernacle of God is with men, and He will dwell with them, and they shall be His people, and God Himself shall be their God" (Rev. 21:3).

Yield: about 8 servings

1 Tbsp. Knox gelatin
¼ cup cold water
4 egg yolks, slightly beaten
¾ cup mild honey
¼ tsp. salt
½ cup lemon juice
1 tsp. grated lemon rind
3 egg whites, stiffly beaten
1 cup whipping cream
1 egg white, stiffly beaten
1 baked 9-inch pastry shell, cooled

Sprinkle the gelatin in the cold water to soften. In the top of a double boiler, combine the slightly beaten egg yolks, ¼ cup of the honey, salt, lemon juice and grated lemon rind. Cook over boiling water, stirring constantly, until the mixture thickens. Add the softened gelatin and stir until it has dissolved. Remove from the heat and cool until the mixture begins to thicken. (You can speed this up by setting the hot pan in a bowl of ice water.) Beat 3 egg whites until stiff, then slowly drizzle in ¼ cup of honey, beating all the while. Fold into the cooled lemon mixture. Turn into a cool, baked pie shell. Chill in the refrigerator for at least two hours until firm. Now beat the remaining one egg white until stiff, then gradually beat in 2 tablespoons of the remaining honey. Whip the cream until stiff in a chilled bowl, while gradually adding two remaining tablespoons of honey. Stir the stiff egg white together with the sweetened whipped cream. Spread on the pie just before serving. A delicious light dessert!

HONEY-OF-AN-APPLE PIE

(Recipe done "kid style")

"But when the Holy Spirit controls our lives he will produce this kind of fruit in us: love, joy, peace, patience, kindness, goodness, faithfulness, gentleness and self-control . . . " (Gal. 5:22-23 TLB).

Oven: 450°   Yield: 6 to 8 servings

Stir together in a small bowl:
- **1 cup white flour**
- **½ cup whole wheat flour**
- **½ tsp. salt**
- **¼ tsp. baking powder**

In another small bowl (be sure the electric beaters are all set up to beat immediately):
- **½ cup shortening**
- **¼ cup boiling water**

Beat until it's fluffy (be careful, it splatters). Now add the flour mixture and mix with the pastry blender (that wirey thing).

Divide the dough in half and roll out between waxed paper (put a tiny bit of flour on the paper first). Carefully place the bottom crust in an 8-inch pie pan.

Apples — wash and slice enough apples to make a rounded measuring quart cup full. (That's the biggest measuring cup)

Stir in ⅓ cup flour and 1 teaspoon cinnamon in the apples until they are all coated. Place the apples in the pie crust.

Then pour ½ cup honey all over the apples.

Put top crust on — pinching the edges together. Put foil around the edges so the edges won't burn. Bake for 40 to 45 minutes 'til it's a nice, light brown color.

It will be yummy!

SOUR CREAM CRANBERRY PIE

"But blessed is the man who trusts in the Lord and has made the Lord his hope and confidence. He is like a tree planted along a riverbank, with its roots reaching deep into the water — a tree not bothered by the heat nor worried by long months of drought. Its leaves stay green and it goes right on producing all its luscious fruit" (Jer. 17:7, 8 TLB).

Oven: 425°, then 375°   Yield: about 8 servings

2 eggs
¾ cup honey
1 cup dairy sour cream
2 Tbsp. cranberry juice
¼ tsp. salt
2 Tbsp. flour
1 cup raw cranberries
1 cup coarsely cut walnuts

Beat the eggs in a small mixing bowl until thick. In another larger mixing bowl mix together the honey, sour cream and cranberry juice. Add the egg mixture and carefully stir in by hand. Mix the salt and flour together with the cranberries. Add to the egg mixture, stirring in gently by hand. Pour into an unbaked 9-inch pie shell. Sprinkle walnuts over the top. Bake for 10 minutes then reduce the heat to 375 degrees and continue baking for 25 minutes more or until well browned. Cool completely before cutting. SOUR CREAM CRANBERRY PIE is a great finale to any November or December meal. That's when fresh cranberries are in season in most areas.

RAISIN PIE

" . . . no mere man has ever seen, heard or even imagined what wonderful things God has ready for those who love the Lord" (1 Cor. 2:9 TLB).

Oven: 425°   Yield: about 8 servings

2 lg. eggs
¾ cup honey
1 cup dairy sour cream
2 Tbsp. orange juice
½ tsp. cinnamon
¼ tsp. salt
2 Tbsp. flour
1 cup raisins
1 cup coarsely chopped walnuts

Here is a wonderfully rich and delicious pie! In a large mixing bowl beat the eggs until thick. In another small mixing bowl combine the honey, sour cream and orange juice. Now fold into the eggs. Mix the cinnamon, salt and flour with the raisins. Stir into the egg mixture. Pour into an unbaked 9-inch pie shell. Sprinkle the coarsely chopped walnuts over the top. Bake for 10 minutes, then turn down the oven to 375 degrees and continue baking for another 25 minutes until nicely browned. Cool before cutting.

THANKSGIVING PUMPKIN PIE

". . . Blessing and glory and majesty and splendor and wisdom and thanks and honor and power and might (be ascribed) to our God to the ages and ages — forever and ever, throughout the eternities of the eternities! Amen! (So be it!)" (Rev. 7:12 TAB).

Oven: 450°   Yield: about 8 servings

1 (9-inch) unbaked pastry shell
½ cup honey
1 cup canned condensed milk
2 cups unsweetened pumpkin puree
4 lg. eggs, beaten
1 tsp. cinnamon
½ tsp. ginger
½ tsp. mace
½ tsp. ground cloves
¾ tsp. salt

Line a 9-inch pie pan with your favorite pastry. Chill in the refrigerator while proceeding to make the filling. Preheat oven. Stir the honey into the canned milk in a thin stream, then stir into the pumpkin puree. Add the eggs, which have been beaten together, and all the seasonings. Stir together until evenly mixed. Pour into the pie shell which you have chilled. Bake for 10 minutes. Then turn down the temperature to 325 degrees and bake for about 40 minutes more or until the filling is set. (A silver knife inserted in the center of the filling should come out clean.) Cool and serve with honey-sweetened whipped cream, spiced with just a touch of cinnamon, if desired.

NO-CRUST PUMPKIN PIE

"For I will restore health unto thee, and I will heal thee of thy wounds, saith the Lord . . . " (Jer. 30:17).

Oven: 325°   Yield: 6 to 8 servings

3 eggs
¾ cup honey
½ tsp. salt
½ tsp. ginger
½ tsp. cinnamon
½ tsp. nutmeg
1¾ cups pumpkin, cooked puree
1 cup evaporated milk

Beat the eggs slightly. Slowly drizzle in the honey, beating all the while. Add the spices, salt and pumpkin. Mix well with your electric mixer. Add the undiluted evaporated milk and beat until well blended and smooth. Rub one teaspoon of butter or margarine into a 9-inch pie pan. Pour the pumpkin mixture into the buttered pan. Bake for about 60 minutes or until done. When it's done a knife blade will come out clean. Allow to cool before serving. Serve with honey-sweetened whipping cream, if desired.

CHRISTMAS PIE

"Now thanks be to God for His Gift, precious beyond telling — His indescribable, inexpressible, free Gift!" (2 Cor. 9:15 TAB).

THE CRUST

¼ cup butter or margarine

¼ cup honey

½ cup carob chips

2 cups cereal (Special K or Rice Crispies)

Melt the butter, honey and carob chips in a saucepan over low heat, stirring constantly until smooth. Remove from heat. Add cereal, stirring until well coated. Gently press the mixture in a buttered 9-inch pie pan to form the crust. Chill.

THE FILLING

4 pkgs. (3 oz. each) cream cheese, softened

½ cup honey

½ cup quartered maraschino cherries

A few halved maraschino cherries

½ cup chopped almonds

2¼ cups whipped cream

In a small mixing bowl, beat the softened cream cheese until smooth. Gradually beat in the honey. Carefully fold in the cherries, almonds and whipped cream. Spread filling in the chilled crust. Garnish with maraschino cherry halves and toasted slivered almonds, if desired. Freeze for at least 4 hours. Ideally, you'll like to make your Christmas pie ahead of time before the last minute bustle of happy holiday activities. Just remember to have it well wrapped or in an air-tight container in your freezer. Remove the CHRISTMAS PIE from the freezer 15 to 30 minutes before serving and let stand at room temperature. Then it will be just perfect to cut and serve as the final course of your Christmas dinner.

Cookies

GRANOLA HONEY DROPS

"My son, eat thou honey, because it is good; and the honeycomb, which is sweet to thy taste" (Prov. 24:13).

Oven: 350°   Yield: 3 dozen

2 cups white flour
¼ tsp. baking soda
¼ tsp. salt
1 tsp. cinnamon
¼ tsp. nutmeg
⅔ cup soft butter or margarine
1 egg
¼ cup honey
1 lg. banana, mashed
2 cups granola

Stir together thoroughly the flour, baking soda, salt, nutmeg and cinnamon in a large mixing bowl. Add the soft butter, egg, honey and mashed banana. Beat together until thoroughly combined. Stir in the granola. Cover and chill the dough for one hour. Drop the dough by rounded teaspoonfuls onto a greased cookie sheet. Bake for 12 to 15 minutes.

HONEY-SPICE CUT-OUT COOKIES

" . . . What things soever ye desire, when ye pray, believe that ye receive them, and ye shall have them" (Mark 11:24).

Oven: 350°   Yield: 3 dozen

½ cup butter or margarine, softened to
**   room temperature**
½ cup honey
2 cups white flour
1 tsp. baking soda
½ tsp. cinnamon
¼ tsp. cloves
¼ tsp. allspice
¼ cup bran flakes cereal, crushed

Cream the softened butter and honey together in a mixing bowl. In another mixing bowl stir together the flour, soda, and spices and mix with the crushed bran flakes. Combine the dry ingredients with the honey and butter. Chill for one hour in the refrigerator. Roll ⅛ inch thick on a floured bread board. You'll need to flour your rolling pin too. Cut out the cookies with a floured cutter. If they stick a little to the board, just use the flat side of a butcher knife to slide them off. Place on an ungreased cookie sheet and sprinkle lightly with just a touch of sugar if desired. Bake for 8 to 10 minutes. Cool on a rack or on paper towels. Makes about 3 dozen delicious cookies.

HONEY PUMPKIN DROPS

"It is a good thing to give thanks unto the Lord, and to sing praises unto thy name, O most High: To shew forth thy lovingkindness in the morning, and thy faithfulness every night" (Ps. 92:1, 2).

Oven: 350°   Yield: 4 dozen

½ cup butter, softened

1 cup honey

2 eggs, beaten

1 cup cooked, mashed pumpkin

2 cups white flour

½ cup whole wheat flour

¼ cup dry milk

1 Tbsp. baking soda

1 tsp. salt

2 tsp. cinnamon

½ tsp. nutmeg

¼ tsp. ginger

1 cup chopped dates

1 cup chopped nuts

Cream the softened butter and honey together in a mixing bowl until light and fluffy. Add the eggs and pumpkin; mix well. Measure out all the dry ingredients (flours, dry milk, baking soda, salt and spices) in a small mixing bowl and stir together. Add the dry ingredients to the honey mixture and stir until blended. Add the chopped dates and nuts and stir in. Drop by heaping teaspoonfuls onto a greased cookie sheet, leaving about two inches between each cookie. Bake in the upper half of your oven for 15 minutes. Remove from cookie sheet immediately and cool on paper towels. These are soft cake-like cookies. The honey helps to keep them moist, as honey does with all baked goods. **HONEY PUMPKIN DROPS** are a perfect way to finish off your children's jack o' lantern. Only you'll want to carve it one night before Halloween and cook it up the morning after Halloween. Another good idea to help keep the pumpkin fresh is to set it outside rather than in a warm house. Don't be afraid to burn a candle inside the pumpkin. You can just carve off the charred area. There will be plenty of pumpkin left!

PEANUT BUTTER CRUNCHIES

"A merry heart doeth good like a medicine: but a broken spirit drieth the bones" (Prov. 17:22).

No bake   Yield: 24-2" squares

1 cup honey

¾ cup peanut butter

5 cups cereal (Special K or Rice Crispies)

1 cup sunflower seeds

In a large, heavy saucepan heat the honey and the peanut butter, stirring constantly till well combined. Now add the cereal and the sunflower seeds and stir till well mixed. Turn out into a buttered 9"x13" pan. Using a buttered spatula or well buttered fingers spread out evenly and press down. When it has cooled cut in 2-inch squares. Guaranteed to be a favorite!

HONEY OATMEAL COOKIES

"Because the Lord is my Shepherd, I have everything that I need" (Ps. 23:1 TLB).

Oven: 350°   Yield: About 4 dozen

¾ cup vegetable oil
1¼ cups honey
2 eggs
2 tsp. vanilla
1 cup finely grated coconut (unsweetened)
½ cup raisins
½ cup chopped walnuts
1½ cups wheat germ
2 cups rolled oats
¾ cup whole wheat flour
1 tsp. salt
¾ cup dry powdered milk

In a large mixing bowl combine the oil, honey, eggs, and vanilla. Beat till thoroughly mixed. Stir in the coconut, raisins, chopped nuts, wheat germ and rolled oats, stirring until evenly blended. In a separate little bowl stir together the whole wheat flour with the dry powdered milk and salt. Add to the cookie dough and stir until the mixture is smooth. Push from a teaspoon onto a greased cookie sheet. Bake for 10 to 12 minutes. Remove hot cookies from the cookie sheet immediately and cool on paper towels. But be sure and watch very carefully. They have a tendency to disappear without much explanation. Was it the Cookie Monster?

CAROB CHIPPERS

"O taste and see that the Lord is good: blessed is the man that trusteth in Him" (Ps. 34:8).

Oven: 325°   Yield: 3 dozen

1 cup soft butter or margarine
½ cup honey
1 tsp. vanilla
½ tsp. salt
1 cup carob chips
½ cup chopped walnuts
1 cup whole wheat flour
1 cup white flour
1 cup dry oatmeal

Cream the softened butter and honey together. Add vanilla and salt and stir. In a separate bowl measure out the flours, oatmeal, carob chips and nuts and stir together. Add to the honey mixture, stirring together until blended. Roll in small balls and place on an ungreased cookie sheet. Flatten each ball with the prongs of a fork. Bake for 15 minutes or until a light golden brown in color. These cookies will store beautifully in a tightly covered container for at least two weeks. Ideal for mailing to that boy in the service, too.

Nature's confectioner, the bee.

John Cleveland, Fuscara

PEPPERNUTS

". . . and if I have not love (God's love in me) I am nothing — a useless nobody" (1 Cor. 13:2 TAB).

Oven: 400°   Yield: about 500 cookies, the size of a nickle

2 cups honey
½ cup butter
1 egg
¾ cup hot water
½ cup finely chopped nuts
1 tsp. cinnamon
¼ tsp. cloves
½ tsp. ginger
1 tsp. baking powder
1 tsp. baking soda
4 cups whole wheat flour
4 cups white flour

Cream together the honey, softened butter and egg. Measure out all the pieces, baking powder, baking soda, and flours and stir together in a separate bowl. Add to the honey mixture and stir till well blended. Add a little more white flour if the dough seems to be sticky. Roll with your hands into long pencil-like sticks ¾" in diameter and freeze overnight between layers of waxed paper. The next day, slice ⅜" thick and place on greased baking sheets so they do not touch each other. Bake for about 12 minutes or until lightly browned. Bake in the upper half of the oven to keep the peppernuts from browning too much on the bottom. They will be hard after they cool. Store in a tightly closed container. The spicy flavor improves with age.

THE ULTIMATE OATMEAL COOKIE

"But thanks be unto God, which giveth us the victory through our Lord Jesus Christ" (1 Cor. 15:57).

Oven: 300°   Yield: about 7 dozen

3 cups old fashioned oatmeal (toasted)
1 cup oatmeal flour
1 cup whole wheat flour
1 cup nonfat dry milk
½ tsp. cloves
2 tsp. cinnamon
1 cup coconut
1 cup dried fruit (raisins, dried apples, apricots)
1 cup walnuts, chopped
1 tsp. salt
4 eggs
1 cup vegetable oil
1 cup honey

Toast the oatmeal in an ungreased skillet over medium heat, stirring constantly. Remove from heat when lightly toasted. Make one cup of oatmeal flour by grinding dry, old-fashioned oatmeal in your blender. In a large mixing bowl mix together the toasted oatmeal, oatmeal flour, whole wheat flour, dry milk, cloves, cinnamon, coconut and salt. Add the chopped nuts and finely chopped dried fruit. Beat the four eggs and set aside. Mix the vegetable oil with the honey and beat well with electric beater. Add the eggs to the honey mixture and beat again. Now mix thoroughly with the dry ingredients. Drop by teaspoonfuls onto a greased cookie sheet. Bake for 20 minutes. This is "The Ultimate Oatmeal Cookie!" Eat 'em any time — for breakfast, lunch or as a snack treat. They're just as nutritious as they are tasty!

NO BAKE APPLE COOKIES

"God is alive! Praise Him who is the great rock of protection" (Ps. 18:46 TLB).

Yield: 4½ dozen

½ cup butter or margarine
1½ cups honey
4 Tbsp. carob powder (or cocoa)
1 cup peeled and grated apple
¼ tsp. salt
3 cups rolled oats
1½ cups finely grated coconut (unsweetened)
1 tsp. vanilla

Melt the butter over low heat in a large saucepan. Add the honey, carob powder, grated apple and salt, stirring till well mixed. Heat to the boiling point, stirring occasionally. Boil for one minute. Remove from the heat and stir in the rolled oats (dry), the coconut and vanilla. Blend well. Drop by teaspoonfuls onto an oiled cookie sheet or oiled waxed paper. When cool, roll in non-instant powdered milk.

SESAME SEED COOKIES

"So don't be anxious about tomorrow, God will take care of your tomorrow too. Live one day at a time" *(Matt. 6:34 TLB).*

Oven: 325°   Yield: 3 dozen

1 cup sesame seeds
½ cup coconut, grated or shredded (sweetened)
2 eggs
½ cup oil
½ cup honey
1 tsp. vanilla
2½ cups whole wheat flour
¼ cup non-instant dry milk
½ tsp. salt

Toast the sesame seeds and the coconut by heating them, unoiled, in a skillet. Stir constantly until evenly toasted a light brown. Remove at once and cool. Blend together thoroughly the eggs, oil, honey and vanilla. Add the toasted seeds and coconut and stir well. Mix the dry ingredients together (flour, dry milk, and salt) and blend in with the honey mixture. Form into balls about 1" in diameter and place on ungreased cookie sheet. Press down with a fork and bake for 15 minutes. These cookies are not as sweet as some. You'll like the rich flavor from the sesame seeds.

HONEY HAYSTACKS

"In Him we live and move and have our being . . ." *(Acts 17:28).*

Oven: 375°   Yield: 3½ dozen

1 cup butter
⅓ cup mild honey
2 small eggs
2½ cups white flour
1 cup angel flaked coconut
½ cup mild honey
¾ tsp. cinnamon

Soften the butter to room temperature. Beat the butter and ⅓ cup of honey together in a mixing bowl. Add the eggs and beat till well blended. Stir in the flour gradually by hand. Shape into balls, using a heaping teaspoon of dough for each ball. Place on an ungreased cookie sheet and bake for 5 minutes. Remove from the oven and make a depression with a thimble or your thumb. Combine the coconut, ½ cup of honey and the cinnamon in a small bowl. Fill the depressions with the coconut mixture. Return to the oven and bake 5 minutes longer. Remove from cookie sheets immediately and cool on wire racks. These dainty little cookies are delicious made with real butter. They will just melt in your mouth. And they're pretty enough to serve with your nicest tea set.

HONEY CUT-OUTS

"Be gentle and ready to forgive; never hold grudges. Remember, the Lord forgave you, so you must forgive others" (Col. 3:13 TLB).

Oven: 375°   Yield: 4 to 5 dozen

1 cup butter, softened to room temperature
½ cup honey
2 hard-boiled egg yolks
1 raw egg
2½ cups white flour
2½ Tbsp. lemon juice
½ tsp. grated lemon rind
¼ tsp. salt
¼ tsp. crushed cardamon seeds, optional

Cream the softened butter together with the honey and egg yolks. Blend well and add all the other ingredients. Stir till mixed thoroughly. Chill the dough for 2 hours and then roll out on a floured bread board until the dough is ⅛ inch thick. You'll need to lightly flour your rolling pin also. Cut out with cookie cutters and place on ungreased cookie sheet. Sprinkle with just a touch of granulated sugar. Bake for 7 or 8 minutes. Makes 4 to 5 dozen cookies depending on the size of cookie cutters. These make good Christmas cookies. Of course, you can decorate them with icing if you desire.

Desserts

FRESH UNCOOKED APPLESAUCE

"And look! I have given you the seed-bearing plants throughout the earth, and all the fruit trees for your food" (Gen. 1:29 TLB).

Yield: 4 to 6 servings

3 lg. apples
½ tsp. salt
1 qt. cold water
1 Tbsp. lemon juice
¼ tsp. cinnamon OR nutmeg
¼ cup honey (or more depending on the tartness
    of apples)

Wash the apples. Cut in half twice, then remove the cores and the seeds. Thinly slice into the salted water. Allow to stand for 15 minutes to prevent discoloration. In your blender, combine the lemon juice, spice and honey with half of the apple slices. Run the blender to mix, adding balance of apples and mixing until all has been blended to as smooth a sauce as desired. Chill before serving. Note: Uncooked applesauce may also be prepared using a medium-sized grater. Of course, the goodness of your applesauce will depend on the freshness and quality of the apples you have to begin with.

PEANUT BUTTER-SESAME BALLS

"Ye are my friends, if ye do whatsoever I command you" (John 15:14).

Yield: 2½ dozen

¾ cup peanut butter
½ cup honey
¾ cup non-instant milk powder
1 cup uncooked rolled oats
¾ cup sesame seeds, toasted
1 tsp. vanilla
1 Tbsp. boiling water
½ cup sesame seeds, toasted

First of all, toast all of the sesame seeds in a dry skillet over medium heat, stirring all the time until the seeds are a light golden brown. Remove from the heat. Now stir together the peanut butter and honey in a mixing bowl. Add the powdered milk, stirring until blended. Next add the rolled oats, ¾ cup sesame seeds, boiling hot water and vanilla. Mix thoroughly. Shape into balls about one inch in diameter. Roll the balls in the ½ cup remaining sesame seeds, coating each ball generously. Refrigerate until firmly set. Then call the kids for a nutritious and tasty snack. Save a few for Dad's lunch box if you can manage.

HONEY SURPRISE MILK BALLS

"He has made everything beautiful in its time; He also has planted eternity in men's heart and mind [a divinely implanted sense of a purpose working through the ages which nothing under the sun, but only God, can satisfy] . . . (Eccles. 3 | TAl

Yiel about 2 dozen

½ cup honey

½ cup peanut butter

1 cup non-instant milk pow 'e

1 cup uncooked rolled oats

½ cup finely grated coconut (unsweetened)

Surprises:

Whole nuts

Glaced cherries

Raisins

Carob-coated peanuts

Carob-coated raisins

Dried fruit of any kind

Carob chips or chocolate chips

Little squares of fresh coconut

Stir the honey and peanut butter together in a small bowl. Add the powdered milk and continue stirring until well-mixed. Add the dry rolled oats, kneading by hand until well blended. Mold the dough into a long roll about 20 inches long and slice with a sharp knife in slices just a little less than an inch. Then make a little hole with your thumb in each slice. Insert the "surprise" nut, candy, dried fruit or whatever. Use your imagination for the surprises. Shape out the dough around the surprise into a ball. Then roll each ball in finely grated coconut if desired. Surprises are fun for the children, especially. And the more variety you come up with, of course, adds to their interest.

HONEY BEE PEANUT BUTTER SANDWICH

"In everything give thanks: for this is the will of God in Christ Jesus concerning you" (1 Thess. 5:18).

Yield: 1 serving

1½ Tbsp. peanut butter

1½ Tbsp. honey

¼ tsp. bee pollen

1 slice bread

Stir the honey and peanut butter together in a little cup with a spoon until well blended. Spread on a slice of your favorite bread. If desired, sprinkle with golden bursts of bee pollen. Serve with a nice cool glass of milk.

BANANA POPSICLES

"And be ye kind one to another, tenderhearted, forgiving one another, even as God for Christ's sake hath forgiven you" (Eph. 4:32).

Yield: 4 popsicles

4 firm bananas
4 wooden sticks
⅓ cup mild-flavored honey
1 pkg. (6 oz.) carob chips or chocolate chips
½ cup peanut butter
¼ cup milk
½ cup walnuts, finely chopped

Peel the firm bananas. Insert wooden sticks in the bananas lengthwise. Chill for one hour in the refrigerator. In a saucepan, combine the honey and carob chips. Stir over low heat until the carob chips are melted. Add the peanut butter. Continue stirring until the mixture comes to a boil. Take off the stove and stir in the milk. Dip the chilled bananas in the mixture to coat. Roll in the finely chopped nuts. Freeze. Fruit must be served frozen.

PEANUT HONEY BARS

1 cup dry powdered milk (non-instant)
1 cup peanut butter
1 cup honey
½ tsp. vanilla
1 cup chopped spanish style peanuts OR
1 cup finely grated coconut

Stir together the powdered milk with the peanut butter and the honey and vanilla. Shape into little rolled bars or bite-sized pieces. Then roll in either the chopped peanuts or the finely grated coconut. Freeze until set firm. Store in the refrigerator. Makes great snacking! And they are so easy to make that even a Kindergarten class might enjoy the project.

ORANGE YOGURT POPSICLES

"The wolf also shall dwell with the lamb, and the leopard shall lie down with the kid: and the calf and the young lion and the fatling together; and a little child shall lead them" (Isa. 11:6).

Yield: 8 popsicles or 12 "cupcakes"

4 cups plain yogurt
1 lg. can frozen orange juice
1 Tbsp. vanilla
¼ cup honey

Mix together the yogurt, frozen orange juice and vanilla until well blended. Warm the honey slightly and add slowly to the cold mixture, stirring all the time. Pour immediately into popsicle molds or little paper cups, using wooden sticks for handles. If you'd like to have some yummy frozen yogurt to serve at the table, try using cupcake papers in your muffin pan. Fill all the way to the top and place in the freezer for at least four hours or until firmly set. To serve the frozen yogurt cupcakes, remove the paper and place upside down in your pretty dessert dishes. The popsicles will be a favorite with children. And what a healthy snack!

FUDGY BROWNIES

"And my God will liberally supply (fill to the full) your every need according to His riches in glory in Christ Jesus"' (Phil. 4:19 TAB).

Oven: 325°   Yield: 16 squares

½ cup butter or margarine
2 1-oz. squares unsweetened chocolate
½ tsp. salt
1 tsp. pure vanilla extract
1 cup mild honey
⅓ cup white flour
1 tsp. baking powder
2 eggs
1 cup coarsely chopped walnuts

Melt the butter, chocolate and salt together in a saucepan over very low heat. Remove from the stove and stir in the vanilla. Then blend in the honey, flour and baking powder. Add the eggs and beat well with an electric mixer. Stir in the coarsely chopped walnuts. Pour into a greased 9"x9"x2" pan and bake for about 35 minutes or until done in the center. Remove from the oven and allow the brownies to cool for 15 minutes, before marking into squares.

Honey is sweet but the bee stings.

George Herbert, Jacula Prudentum.

SESAME HONEY CANDY

Yield: 2½ dozen balls

¼ cup butter or margarine
½ cup sesame seeds
1 cup finely grated coconut, unsweetened
½ tsp. vanilla
¼ cup honey

Melt the butter in a heavy saucepan over low heat. Stir in the sesame seeds and coconut and continue cooking for 5 minutes. Take the pan off the heat and add the honey and vanilla, mixing well. Cool until the dough is stiff enough to shape into balls. (Takes about 20 minutes in the freezer, if you transfer it into another cool container.) When the dough is stiff, roll into little balls about one inch in diameter. Store in the refrigerator until ready to eat. Another nice extra thing about making Sesame Honey Candy is the softening beauty treatment you give your hands in the process!!

BANANA MANNA

"Bodily exercise is all right, but spiritual exercise is much more important and is a tonic for all you do" *(1 Tim. 4:8 TLB).*

Yield: 2 servings

2 lg. bananas
2 Tbsp. honey
½ tsp. bee pollen

Peel and slice two large bananas in round slices, in two sauce dishes. Drizzle a tablespoonful of honey over each serving. Then top it off with a sprinkling of golden pollen. Mmmmmm. Thanks to the bees!

MANNA BARS

1 cup honey
1 cup peanut butter
½ tsp. pure vanilla
1 cup dry powdered milk (non-instant)
½ cup bee pollen

Cream the honey and peanut butter together. Then stir in the vanilla and the powdered milk, stirring until well-blended. Chill in the refrigerator for at least ½ hour. Shape into little bite-sized nuggets or any shape that resembles a candy bar. Roll in bee pollen. Freeze until firmly set. Here is a truly nutritious energy food!

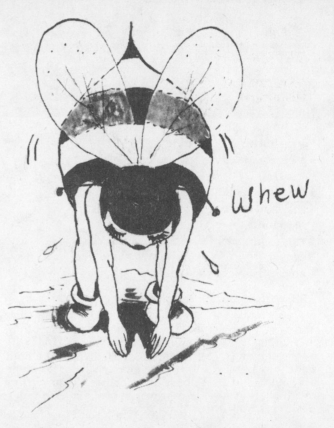

MINT FRUIT DIP

"And whatever you do or say, let it be as a representative of the Lord Jesus, and come with him into the presence of God the Father to give him your thanks" (Col. 3:17 TLB).

⅓ cup apple cider vinegar

1 Tbsp. lemon juice

1 cup mild honey

⅛ tsp. mint extract

1 tsp. finely grated onion

¼ tsp. salt

1 tsp. poppy seed (or celery seed)

1 tsp. paprika

1 tsp. dry mustard

2 or 3 drops of green food coloring

1 cup salad oil

Here's a good idea for your next party. Serve a platter of fresh fruit, sliced and cut in different interesting shapes. You might like to include celery also. Let your guests spice up the fruit with MINT FRUIT DIP.

In your blender, or with an electric mixer, mix all the ingredients together, except for the salad oil. Mix until well blended. Then add the salad oil, pouring in very slowly, and mixing well as you go. When the mixture has reached a smooth consistency pour into a glass jar and let stand for several hours in the refrigerator for the flavors to blend. Serve chilled. Keep any left over dip in the refrigerator with the lid on.

BANANA-FRUIT LEATHER

"Jesus answered and said unto him, If a man love me he will keep my words: and my Father will love him, and we will come unto him, and make our abode with him" (John 14:23).

Oven: warm, approx. 100°

6 very ripe bananas

¼ cup honey

¼ inch slice of lemon

Peel the ripe bananas and place them all in your blender. Process until they are pureed. Add the honey and slice of lemon and process again until thoroughly blended. Pour the mixture out onto 2 large cookie sheets that you have lined with plastic wrap. Carefully spread the banana mixture out evenly with the back side of a large spoon. Place in a warm oven or any warm place that's approximately 100 degrees. Of course, if you have a food dehydrator, this is most ideal. At 100 degrees it will take from 12 to 14 hours until the leather is ready. It should not feel the least bit sticky to the touch. When it's done, roll into small rolls, then cut into desired sized pieces with your kitchen shears. Fruit leather is a good, healthy snack food. Ideal for lunch boxes and the back-packers knapsack.

Variations: You can make banana-berry leather using half as many berries as banana. Try blackberries, raspberries, or strawberries. Sweeten with honey to your taste. It's best if you remove the seeds from the berry puree before blending with the bananas.

ENERGY BARS

"But the Lord is faithful; He will make you strong and guard you from satanic attacks of every kind" (2 Thess. 3:3 TLB).

Yield: about 3 dozen bars

1 cup carob powder
1 cup non-instant powdered milk
1½ cups finely grated coconut, unsweetened
¼ cup bee pollen
¼ cup chopped raisins
¼ cup chopped dry apples
¼ cup toasted sesame seeds
¼ cup toasted sunflower seeds
⅓ cup oil
1½ cup honey
Dash of allspice
Dash of cardamon
2 to 3 cups chopped almonds or filberts

In a large mixing bowl stir together the carob powder, powdered milk, coconut, bee pollen, chopped raisins and chopped dry apples. Add the toasted sesame seeds and the toasted sunflower seeds (which you have lightly toasted in an unoiled skillet, stirring constantly over medium heat). Stir in with the other dry ingredients. Blend the honey and oil together in a small bowl with your mixer. Add to the dry ingredients. You may need to use your hands to get the candy evenly mixed. A dash of allspice and also a dash of cardamon will add just the right flavor. Allow the mixture to cool in the refrigerator for at least an hour. Then form into little bars or bite-sized pieces, rolling each one in chopped almonds or chopped filberts. Keep handy in the refrigerator for a quick snack. They'll be a hit with any joggers in your family!

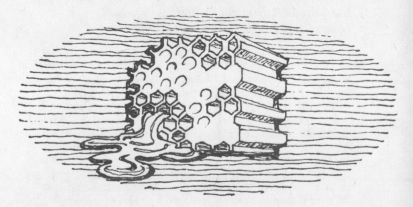

COCONUT CREAM POM POMS

"As the mountains are round about Jerusalem, so the Lord is round about His people from henceforth even for ever" (Ps. 125:2).

Yield: about 2 dozen

1 pkg. (8 oz.) cream cheese
¼ cup honey
⅓ cup chopped walnuts
1 cup finely shredded, unsweetened coconut
Dash of salt

Allow the cream cheese to soften to room temperature. Then cream together the honey and creamed cheese with an electric beater till light and fluffy. Stir in ⅓ cup of the coconut, the chopped nuts and the salt. Chill in your freezer for about 20 minutes, or in the refrigerator for one hour. Shape into balls, using a rounded teaspoonful of dough for each ball. Roll the balls in the remaining ⅔ cup of coconut. Chill in the refrigerator at least two hours before serving. This candy is outstanding in flavor, yet very easy to make. It seems to "show off" the honey flavor instead of just the sweetness you get from sugar. We enjoy it with MAPLE HONEY — our first honey of the spring in the Northwest.

HOMEMADE HONEY ICE CREAM

"How sweet are thy words unto my taste! yea, sweeter than honey to my mouth!" (Ps. 119:103).

Yield: 1 gallon

1 qt. milk
1 qt. heavy cream
1¾ cups honey
1 Tbsp. vanilla
6 egg whites
6 egg yolks

In saucepan, combine milk, cream, and honey. Heat to lukewarm over low heat, stirring constantly. Stir in the vanilla. Chill. Beat the egg whites until stiff. Then in another small bowl beat the egg yolks until thick. Now carefully blend the whites and yolks. Fold them into the milk mixture. Pour this into your ice cream freezer and crank away, following the directions that came with your freezer. When fresh fruits are in season, you can fill the ice cream freezer up only ⅔ full; then about halfway through the freezing process add your chilled fruit and continue cranking. When the ice cream is done, remove dasher, and return to freezer for at least an hour to set completely, if you can wait that long. Homemade ice cream is such a special treat! Don't save it only for the Fourth of July.

HONEY BEE AMBROSIA

"For God hath not given us the spirit of fear; but of power, and of love, and of a sound mind" (2 Tim. 1:7).

Yield: 6 servings

4 med. oranges
2 bananas
½ cup orange juice
¼ cup mild honey
2 Tbsp. lemon juice
¼ cup flaked coconut

Peel the oranges, then with a very sharp knife slice thinly into a large bowl. Peel the bananas, cut in thin round slices into the bowl with the oranges and toss together. In a small bowl, blend the orange juice together with the honey and lemon juice, using your electric mixer. Pour over the freshly sliced fruit. Spoon into dessert glasses. Sprinkle each serving with a little flaked coconut. Keep chilled in the refrigerator until ready to serve. This is a quick and easy dessert that is nice to serve with any meal. Low in calories too!

STEAMED CARROT PUDDING WITH ORANGE SAUCE

"And we know that all things work together for good to them that love God, to them who are the called according to His purpose" (Rom. 8:28).

Yield: 8 servings

½ cup butter or margarine
⅓ cup honey
1 cup whole wheat flour
½ tsp. cloves
1 tsp. nutmeg
1 tsp. cinnamon
1 tsp. allspice
1 tsp. baking soda
½ tsp. baking powder
1 cup grated carrots
1 cup grated potatoes
1 cup chopped walnuts
2 Tbsp. water

Stir the butter and honey together in a sauce pan over low heat until blended. Remove from heat. Measure all the dry ingredients together in a small bowl and stir to mix well. Set aside. Grate the carrots and the potatoes, then stir them together with the chopped walnuts and the water. Now stir the honey mixture in with the dry ingredients until blended. Then stir in the carrot mixture, stirring only enough to evenly mix. Put the pudding mixture into a greased 3-lb. shortening can. Put a piece of foil over the top and tie it down securely with a piece of string. Place the can on a rack in a large kettle. Fill the kettle until the water level is half-way up on the shortening can. Simmer slowly with the lid on for about 3 to 3½ hours. Remove from heat and allow to cool for 15 minutes before removing from the can. Serve with hot orange sauce.

ORANGE SAUCE

¼ cup butter or margarine
¼ cup mild honey
1 cup orange juice
½ cup water
1½ Tbsp. cornstarch
1 Tbsp. grated orange peel
Dash of salt

Stir the honey and butter together in a small saucepan over low heat until well-blended. Stir the cornstarch into the cold water, then into the orange juice. Add to the honey mixture and continue cooking over low heat till the sauce thickens. Stir in the orange peel and salt and serve hot over the fresh steamed pudding.

Canning with Honey

"As the rain and snow come down from heaven and stay upon the ground to water the earth, and cause the grain to grow and to produce seed for the farmer and bread for the hungry so also is my Word. I send it out and it always produces fruit. . . " (Isa. 55:10,11 TLB).

Select fruit in its top quality. The quality of your canned goods will, of course, be related to the choice of fruit you put in the jar. Peaches, pears, apricots, cherries and plums have all been successfully canned with honey in our kitchen. Be sure to select the mildest honey available, definitely not clover. We have found that fruits canned with honey retain more of the fresh fruit taste. They can be enjoyed all year 'round.

COLD PACK your fruit firmly into your jars, but do not crush. Make sure your jars and lids have all been sterilized. It pays to take every precaution for spotless cleanliness when canning. It's nice to work with a helper, too, to handle the job as quickly as possible, without the fruit browning. If you are working alone use Fruit Fresh according to direction to prevent browning. Pour the boiling hot syrup over the cold packed fruit, leaving ½ inch of head space at the top of the jar.

The sweetness of the syrup is a matter of personal taste. First boil the water. Then remove from heat and stir in the honey till dissolved.

LIGHT SYRUP — 1 cup honey to 4 cups water
MEDIUM SYRUP — 2 cups honey to 4 cups water
HEAVY SYRUP — 3 cups honey to 4 cups water

After filling the jars with hot syrup, immediately tighten down the lids as firmly as possible. Process in a hot water canner. Begin timing as soon as the water boils. Cooking times are as follows:

Apricots — 30 minutes
Peaches — 30 minutes
Pears — 30 minutes
Plums — 25 minutes
Cherries — 20 minutes

(These times are for canning in quart jars. If you are using pints, decrease the time by 5 minutes.)

FROZEN BLACKBERRY JUICE

"... The Father hath not left me alone; for I do always those things that please Him" (John 8:29).

Yield: 1 quart juice

4 quarts blackberries
1 Tbsp. lemon juice
⅓ cup light, mild honey

Place the berries in a strainer and rinse under cold, running water. Then process about one cup of berries at a time in your blender until they are pureed. Pour the pureed berries into a jelly bag. (You can buy good strong jelly bags at a wine supply store.) Don your rubber gloves and squeeze out the juice. Pour the juice into your blender again and add the lemon juice and honey, processing until the honey is blended in. Pour into clean milk cartons to freeze. Leave enough room for the juice to expand as it freezes — about 1½ inches. Staple the top of the carton together and put in your deep freeze. Allow to thaw in the refrigerator before using.

In Western Washington we are blessed with an abundance of native berries, the most prolific being our Evergreen and Himalayan blackberries. They are free for the picking along country roadsides and fences. Be sure to go to an unsprayed area. Wear an old long-sleeved shirt because there are lots of stickers! The berries are worth it, though. Pick enough to eat fresh as well as enough to "put away" in frozen blackberry juice.

EASY GRAPE JUICE

"... The vine shall yield her fruit, and the ground shall give its increase, and the heavens shall give their dew... " (Zech. 8:12 TAB).

Concord grapes
Boiling water
Honey

Wash the grapes, discarding the stems. Scald your quart canning jars. Fill each jar with one cup of grapes, topped with one tablespoon of mild honey. Cover the grapes with boiling water. Screw on the lids tightly and process in a hot water cooker-canner for just 10 minutes. Remove from the canner and place the jars on a turkish towel in the cabinet, away from any draft. After they have sealed and cooled, store away in your fruit cellar or cupboard for at least six weeks. After the juice has aged, simply pour through a strainer or a colander and you'll have the most delicious grape juice in your life! It's almost too simple to be true, but we've been putting up grape juice like this for years and it works every time. Just make sure the grapes are nice and ripe.

FROZEN PEACHES 'N HONEY

"Thy words were found, and I did eat them; and thy word was unto me the joy and rejoicing of mine heart: for I am called by thy name, O Lord God of hosts" (Jer. 15:16).

Figure about two pounds of fresh peaches for every quart container. Select fully ripe peaches in top condition. Make your syrup ahead of time and have it chilled in the refrigerator before using. The sweetness of the syrup is a matter of personal taste. Choose between the thin or medium syrup recipes.

Thin Syrup
Blend one cup of mild honey to three cups of very hot water. Chill before using.

Medium Syrup
Blend two cups of mild flavored honey in 2 cups of very hot water. Chill before using. (Our favorite honey for "putting up" peaches is Huckleberry Honey.)

Wash the peaches. Work in small quantities unless you have a good helper. Blanch in boiling water for one minute. Cool immediately in ice cold water. Have some extra ice frozen up ahead of time. Slip the skin off one peach at a time. Remove pit and slice directly into your freezer carton, containing chilled syrup. Place a crumpled piece of aluminum foil on top to keep the peaches under the syrup — this will prevent browning. Put the lid on immediately and get it right into the deep freezer. Thaw out about half-way before serving. Delicious!

Mine be a cot beside the hill;
A beehive's hum shall soothe my ear;
A willowy brook that turns a mill,
With many a fall shall linger near.

Samuel Rogers (1763-1855)

APPLE JELLY

"The Lord will give strength unto His people: the Lord will bless His people with peace" (Ps. 29:11).

Yield: 12 oz. jar

6-oz. can frozen apple juice (unsweetened)
1 cup water
2 Tbsp. honey
3 Tbsp. agar-agar flakes

Empty the frozen apple juice concentrate into a small saucepan. Add the water, honey and agar-agar flakes. Stir and boil with a slow boil for 15 minutes, stirring constantly. Pour in a jelly jar and let stand until it cools and jells. Store in the refrigerator and eat right away. For the best results, use one of the berry honeys, such as blackberry honey, huckleberry honey, or snowberry honey.

Note: If you are cooking for someone who is on a restricted diet with no sugar or honey at all, you can make this apple jelly leaving out the honey. Apples are quite sweet in themselves; you'll be surprised just how sweet.

Oh, for a bee's experience
Of clovers and of noon!

Emily Dickinson, Poems

HONEY BEE SUNSHINE PRESERVES

"But unto you that fear my name shall the Sun of righteousness arise with healing in his wings..." (Mal. 4:2).

Yield: 5 or 6 jelly glasses

4 cups cubed peaches
4 cups sliced apricots
2 cups cubed papaya
½ cup fresh orange juice
2 cups honey (the mildest available)
¼ cup tapioca flour
½ cup water

Combine the peaches, apricots, papaya and orange juice in a heavy saucepan. Stir in the honey and cook over medium-low heat about 15 minutes, stirring occasionally. Remove from heat and add the tapioca flour which has been combined with ½ cup water. Return to the stove and cook to the desired consistency. Pour into sterile jelly glasses or jars. Put one in the refrigerator to use right away. The rest may be put in the freezer for later use. Store any opened jars of HONEY BEE SUNSHINE PRESERVES in the refrigerator.

OLD-FASHIONED PEAR BUTTER

"But the path of the just is as the shining light, that shineth more and more unto the perfect day" (Prov. 4:18).

Yield: 5 pints

6 pounds pears, ripe
(2½ qts. when pureed)
2 cups honey
15¼ oz. can crushed pineapple
1 tsp. cinnamon
½ tsp. cloves, ground
½ tsp. ginger, ground

Wash and core the fully ripened pears. Peel if desired — I prefer to leave the peeling on. It's a little grainier textured but the flavor can't be beat! Puree the pear halves, a few at a time, in your blender. Place the pureed pears in a large heavy saucepan and stir together with the honey, crushed pineapple, and spices. Cook down about 1 inch, simmering slowly. This will take about 4 hours. Stir occasionally. Pour in hot sterile jars and seal.

FRESH ORANGE MARMALADE

"... The time of the singing of birds is come — and the voice of the turtle is heard in our land" (S. of S. 2:12).

Yield: about 4 8-oz. jelly jars

2 oranges
½ lemon
¾ cup water
1 envelope Knox gelatin in ¼ cup cold water
6-oz. can frozen pineapple juice concentrate
1 cup mild flavored honey
½ cup frozen orange juice concentrate

Wash and peel two oranges and ½ lemon, leaving most of the white membrane on the fruit. Now find a good comfortable spot to sit down in your kitchen and cut all the peel from the oranges and ½ lemon into very tiny slices using your kitchen shears. I like to sit down with the bowl in my lap, like my Grandmother used to do for this task. You should come up with about 1½ cups of tiny slices of citrus peel. Place in a saucepan with ¾ cup of water. Bring to a boil over medium heat, stirring occasionally. Then cover, turn to low heat, and simmer 10 to 15 minutes or until tender. Now with a very sharp knife (or an electric slicing knife) slice the oranges into thin slices, cutting crosswise. Carefully divide the slices into little pieces between each membrane. Keep any juice that you may lose. Of course, the sharper the knife, the less juice

you'll lose. Soak the Knox gelatin in ¼ cup of cold water. When the peel is tender, add the frozen pineapple juice and bring to a good boil again. Remove from heat and stir in the softened gelatin, stirring until it dissolves. Stir in the honey and the orange slices, which you have prepared along with the orange juice concentrate. Mix well. Chill until the gelatin begins to set. Then stir to distribute the orange peel and sections. Fill jelly glasses or jars, or else use little soft margarine tubs. Put one in your refrigerator for ready use and the rest in the freezer.

STRAWBERRY FREEZER JAM

"But seek ye first the kingdom of God, and His righteousness; and all these things shall be added unto you" (Matt. 6:33).

Yield: 2½ pints

4 cups mild flavored honey
2¾ cups mashed strawberries (about 5 cups fresh berries)
¼ cup fresh lemon juice
1 (2-oz.) pkg. powdered jam and jelly pectin

This delicious jam captures all the flavor of June's freshly harvested strawberries, because there is no cooking at all. Carefully select each red ripe berry, removing the stems and placing in a large strainer or colander. Discard any berries that are not in top condition. Rinse in cold running water, shaking off all the excess water. Place in a bowl and mash with a potato masher, leaving some of the berries in larger pieces if desired. Stir in the lemon juice. Slowly **sift** in the powdered pectin, stirring vigorously. Let stand at room temperature for 30 minutes, stirring occasionally. Add the honey and mix well. Pour into freezer containers. (Save your little margarine tubs — they work beautifully.) Chill at least 24 hours in below zero freezer. Opened jars must be kept in the refrigerator.

Variations: To make RASPBERRY FREEZER JAM omit the lemon juice and use 3 cups of mashed raspberries.

For BLACKBERRY FREEZER JAM follow the same recipe as in strawberry freezer jam.

By planning our work
And working our plans,
We gather more honey
And stay out of jams.

Author unknown

CREAMED APRICOT JAM

" . . . It shall be in thy mouth sweet as honey" (Rev. 10:9).

Yield: 2 cups

½ lb. dried apricots
Water
½ cup creamed honey

Place the dried apricots in a bowl and cover with cold water. Allow to soak from 4 to 6 hours or until the water has been absorbed. The time will vary because not all apricots have been dried to the same degree or by the same process. When the dried apricots are soft but yet holding their shape, they are ready. Cut up enough apricots in very small pieces to make ⅓ cup; set aside. Put the rest through a meat grinder using a medium blade, or process a few at a time in your blender, making the apricots into a puree. Now stir ½ cup of creamed honey together with the apricot puree and the ⅓ cup of finely chopped apricots. No cooking is required at all! But remember, you must use creamed honey — not liquid honey. Fill 2 jelly glasses. Put one in the refrigerator to use right away and the other in the freezer for later use.

Note: Try other types of dried fruit for more yummy uncooked jams!

CANNED SPAGHETTI SAUCE

"To enjoy your work and to accept your lot in life — that is indeed a gift from God" (Eccles. 5:20 TLB).

Yield: about 10 pints

6 qts. chopped tomatoes

2 qts. chopped onions

3 green peppers, chopped

2 little red hot peppers, chopped

2 Tbsp. garlic, minced

2 Tbsp. oregano leaves

1½ bay leaves

1 tsp. whole cloves

1 Tbsp. celery seed

1 Tbsp. black peppercorns

1 inch stick cinnamon

¼ cup honey

3 - 303 cans mushrooms (pieces & stems),
    drained — optional

2 Tbsp. salt

1 cup apple cider vinegar

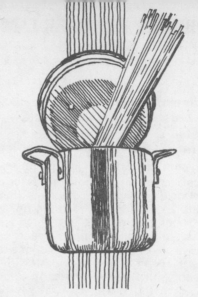

Simmer the chopped tomatoes with the onions, peppers and garlic in your largest pan. (Your canning kettle will work just fine.) Stir frequently to prevent from scorching and simmer until the onions are tender. Remove from heat. Ladle out about 2 cups of the hot tomato mixture at a time and puree in your blender until smooth. Continue until you have pureed the entire mixture. Return to the heat and stir in the honey and the salt. Tie all the spices in a little cotton bag and add to the hot mixture. Simmer slowly for 3 to 4 hours, stirring frequently. Remove the spice bag when the sauce reaches the spiciness you desire. Add the 3 cans of drained mushrooms and simmer for about 30 more minutes. After the sauce has reached its desired consistency stir in the apple cider vinegar and cook for only 10 more minutes. Pour the spaghetti sauce into hot sterilized jars, filling up to ¼ inch from the top. Seal.

TOMATO CATSUP

"As the rain and snow come down from heaven and stay upon the ground to water the earth, and cause the grain to grow and to produce seed for the farmer and bread for the hungry, so also is my word. I send it out and it always produces fruit . . . (Isa. 55:10 TLB).

Yield: about 4 quarts

6 qts. chopped tomatoes
2 qts. chopped onions
3 red peppers, cut up
2 Tbsp. minced garlic
1½ bay leaves
1 Tbsp. whole cloves
1 Tbsp. celery seed
1 Tbsp. black peppercorns
2 inches stick cinnamon
½ cup honey
2 Tbsp. salt
1 cup apple cider vinegar

Simmer the chopped tomatoes with the onions, pepper and garlic in a large pan. We use our canning kettle. Stir frequently and simmer until the onions are tender. Remove from heat. Ladle out about 2 cups of the hot tomato mixture at a time and puree until smooth in your blender. Continue until you have pureed the entire mixture. Return to the heat and stir in the honey and the salt. Tie all the spices in a little cotton bag and add to the hot mixture. Simmer slowly for 3 to 4 hours, stirring occasionally. Cook until the catsup has boiled down about 1" in the pan and has thickened sufficiently. Add the apple cider vinegar and simmer for about 10 more minutes. Remove the spice bag. Pour the catsup into sterilized bottles and seal.

ZUCCHINI PICKLE RELISH

"Yes, the Lord pours down His blessings on the land and it yields its bountiful crops" (Ps. 87:12 TLB).

Yield: about 4 pints

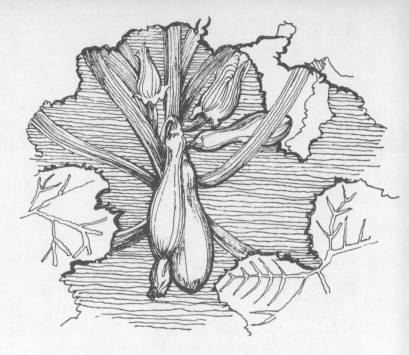

2 lbs. zucchini, finely chopped
1 green pepper, finely chopped
2 sm. dry onions, finely chopped
¼ cup salt
1¾ cup mild honey
1½ cup vinegar
1 Tbsp. mixed pickling spice
1 tsp. mustard seed
½ cinnamon stick

Wash and chop the zucchini, green pepper and onions. Stir together in either a large glass or stainless steel bowl. (Or better yet, use a crock, if you have one.) Sprinkle the salt evenly over the top and let stand for about 4 hours. While the brine mixture is standing make your pickling syrup by boiling together the honey, vinegar and spices. Stir and boil gently for 5 minutes. Remove from heat and let stand while the vegetables are soaking in the salt brine. When the 4 hours are up drain the vegetables **well** in a colander. Strain all the spices out of the syrup. Combine the vegetables and strained syrup and boil for 10 to 12 minutes. Pack the hot relish in sterilized pint jars. Screw down with boiling hot lids as tightly as possible. Place the hot jars of Zucchini Pickle Relish on a turkish towel on your counter to cool and seal. When you hear a little "pop" you'll know they have sealed. Store them in a cool place; a shelf in your garage or basement would do nicely. Enjoy ZUCCHINI PICKLE RELISH with hamburgers or as an accompaniment to any meat dish.

WATERMELON PICKLES

"For as surely as the earth brings forth its shoots, and as a garden causes what is sown in it to spring forth, so surely the Lord God will cause righteousness and justice and praise to spring forth before all the nations (through the self-fulfilling power of His word)" (Isa. 61:11 TAB).

Yield: 3 pints

2 lbs. watermelon rind, trimmed (about 6 cups)
2 cups honey
2 lemons
2 sticks cinnamon
2 tsp. whole cloves
1 oz. fresh ginger root
2 Tbsp. salt in 1 qt. water
1½ cups water
1½ cups vinegar

Use a thick watermelon. Trim away all the red part and the dark green part of the rind. Cut the rind into small chunks or rounds if you desire. Make a brine by dissolving the salt in a quart of water. Whenever making pickles be sure not to use the iodized salt. We use sea salt with good success. Soak the watermelon rind in the brine solution overnight. The next morning remove from the salt water and cook in clear water until tender for about 10 minutes. Drain. Make a spice bag from cheesecloth and add the cinnamon, cloves and gingerroot. Chop the lemons. Place lemons, 1½ cups water, 1½ cups vinegar and the spice bag in a large saucepan and bring to a boil. Turn down heat and add the honey. Now add the drained watermelon rind. Simmer until the pickles are clear and transparent (takes about 30 minutes). Remove the spice bag and seal pickles in hot sterilized jars. Allow only ¼-inch headspace in each jar. Note: If mixture gets too thick before the pickles become transparent a small amount of boiling water may be added.

Index

THIS 'N THAT

Forward 8
Flavors of Honey 9
More about Honey. 10
Know Your Ingredients 12
Oven Temperatures 16
Temperature Conversions 16
Metric Symbols 16
Metric Conversion Table 17

BREAKFAST

Apple Muesli. 23
Fresh Fruit Toppings. 22
Granola Deluxe. 19
Honey Butter. 20
Honey Butter Whip 19
Honey Cinnamon Toast 20
Honey Maple Syrup. 24
Hot Honeyed Grapefruit 25
Marilyn's Homemade Granola. 21
Poppy Seed Honey Toast 25

Sourdough Pancakes 24
Trailside Breakfast 23

BEVERAGES

Carob Mint Smoothie 32
Citrus Sparkle 27
Deep Sleep Tea 28
Eggnog 31
Energy Drink. 31
Honeyed Chocolate 31
Honey Ice Cubes 33
Lemonade 33
Nightcaps for Two 33
Orange Julie 27
Slush Punch 29
Spiced Tea Special. 30
Strawberry Smoothie 28

BREADS

A+ Sourdough Bread 40
Applesauce Nut Bread. 36
Bagels 43
Banana Bread 38
Barley Loaves 52
Bran Muffins. 36
Cracked Wheat Bread 35

Cranberry Honey Loaf 42
Cream 'N Honey Wheat Bread 39
Grandma's Little Honey Buns 53
Hamburger Buns 44
Honey Dill Batter Bread 45
Honey-Orange Rye Bread 48
Joyce's Surprise Sandwich Bread 37
100% Whole Wheat Bread 51
Peanut Bread 48
Sourdough 40
Sourdough English Muffins 50
Whole Wheat Potato Bread 47
Zucchini Bread 46

SALADS & DRESSINGS

Apricot-Honey Dressing 63
Crab Louis 56
Five Bean Salad 59
French Dressing 57
Fresh Spinach Salad 60
Garden Green Salad 57
Harvestime Salad 62
Honey-Citrus Gelatin 62
Honey Cream Dressing 62
Honey-of-a-Dressing 60
Louis Dressing 56

Molded Blueberry Salad 64
Old-Fashioned Rhubarb Sauce 65
Orange-Honey French Dressing 61
Poppy Seed Dressing 55
Raw Cranberry Relish 65
Russian Salad Dressing 61
Sauerkraut Salad 58
Spinach-Cashew Salad 60
Summer Salad 63
Tabbouli Salad 58
Watercress Tossed Salad 55

MEATS & VEGETABLES

Autumn Apple Pork Chops 78
Baked Acorn Squash 75
Baked Lentils with Honey 72
Borsch 77
Chicken Teriyaki 70
Chicken with a Difference 79
Curried Cabbage and Meatballs 79
Festive Mexican Tamale Pie 69
Garbanzo Meatball Stew 73
Harvard Beets 76
Holiday Ham with Honey-Orange Glaze 76
Honey Baked Beans 72
Honeyed Parsnips 71

Jane's Beef Teriyaki 68
Kidney Beans Supreme 75
Lasagne. 71
Macaroni and Cheese 78
Minted Carrots 73
Minted Lamp Chops 68
Spareribs with Barbecue Sauce 74
Sweet 'N Sour Pork 67
Sweet 'N Sour Sauce 67

CAKES

Adam and Eve's Honey-of-a-Fig Cake 88
Banana Spice Cake 88
Carob-Chip Zucchini Cake. 86
Carrot Cake. 81
Coconut Frosting. 81
Cranberry Cheese Cake 87
Easy Orange Frosting 83
Gingerbread 82
Honey Buttercream Icing. 88
Honey-Carob Cake 84
Honey Cream Icing 85
Honey-of-a-Fig Cake Glaze 89
Lemon Cottage Cheese Cake 89
Orange Honey Cake. 82
Quick Honey Pecan Icing. 84

Sourdough Carob Cake 85

PIES

Christmas Pie 99
Coconut Pie Shell. 94
Fresh Strawberry Pie 92
Honey-of-an-Apple Pie 96
Lemon Chiffon Pie. 95
Mile High Banana Pie 92
No-Crust Pumpkin Pie. 98
One Crust Rhubarb Pie 91
Pecan Pie. 91
Raisin Pie 97
Sour Cream Cranberry Pie 97
Strawberry Cream Freezer Pie 94
Thanksgiving Pumpkin Pie 98
Wild Blackberry Pie. 93

COOKIES

Carob Chippers 103
Granola Honey Drops 101
Honey Cut-Outs. 107
Honey Haystacks 106
Honey Oatmeal Cookies. 103
Honey Pumpkin Drops 102
Honey Spice Cut-Out Cookies 101

No-Bake Apple Cookies 105
Peanut Butter Crunchies 102
Peppernuts 104
Sesame Seed Cookies 106
Ultimate Oatmeal Cookies 105

DESSERTS

Banana Fruit Leather 115
Banana Manna 114
Banana Popsicles 111
Coconut Cream Pom Poms 117
Energy Bars 116
Fresh Uncooked Applesauce 109
Fudgy Brownies 113
Homemade Honey Ice Cream 117
Honey Bee Ambrosia 118
Honey Bee Peanut Butter Sandwiches 110
Honey Surprise Milk Balls 110
Manna Bars 114
Mint Fruit Dip 115
Orange Sauce 119
Orange Yogurt Popsicles 112
Peanut Butter Sesame Balls 109
Peanut Honey Bars 112
Sesame Honey Candy 113
Steamed Carrot Pudding with Orange Sauce 119

CANNING WITH HONEY

Apple Jelly 124
Canned Spaghetti Sauce 128
Creamed Apricot Jam 127
Easy Grape Juice 122
Fresh Orange Marmalade 126
Frozen Blackberry Juice 122
Frozen Peaches 'N Honey 123
Honey Bee Sunshine Preserves 125
Old-Fashioned Pear Butter 125
Strawberry Freezer Jam 127
Tomato Catsup 129
Watermelon Pickles 131
Zucchini Pickle Relish 130

Your Notes About Honey